FLORIDA STATE
UNIVERSITY LIBRARIES

SEP 8 1999

TALLAHASSEE, FLORIDA

SUN YAT-SEN IN HAWAII

SIX ERAS OF DR. SUN AFTER IOLANI AND PUNAHOU

1890
24 years old

Medical student in Hong Kong Determined to bring change in China

1911
45 years old

Provisional President of the Republic of China

1895
29 years old

Founding Hsing Chung Hui Started uprisings against the Manchu Government

1918
52 years old

Striving to unify China and establish a democratic government

1905
39 years old

Forming the Tung Meng Hui Continue organizing uprisings

1924
58 years old

Exerting himself to the utmost trying to Unify China Suffered serious liver disease in Tanjin

SUN'S DYING WORDS
PEACE, STRUGGLE, SAVE CHINA

Drawings by Raymond Mun Kong Lum

Sun Yat-sen in Hawaii

Activities and Supporters

Yansheng Ma Lum
Raymond Mun Kong Lum

Hawaii Chinese History Center · Honolulu
and
Dr. Sun Yat-sen Hawaii Foundation · Honolulu

© 1999 Yansheng M. Lum
All rights reserved
Printed in the United States of America
04 03 02 01 00 99   5 4 3 2 1

Library of Congress Cataloging-in-Publication Data
Lum, Yansheng Ma, 1925–
　　Sun Yat-sen in Hawaii : activities and supporters / Yansheng Ma
Lum, Raymond Mun Kong Lum.
　　　p.　　cm.
　　Includes bibliographical references and index.
　　ISBN 0-8248-2254-4 (cloth : alk. paper)
　　ISBN 0-8248-2179-3 (pbk. : alk. paper)
　　　1. Sun, Yat-sen, 1866–1925.   2. Chinese—Hawaii—History.
　3. Chinese—Hawaii—Biography.   4. China—History—
　1861–1912.
　　I. Lum, Raymond Mun Kong.   II. Title.
　　DS777.L86   1999
　　951.04′1′092—dc21
　　[B]   99–20725
　　　　　　　　　　　　　　　　　　　　　　　　　　　　　　CIP

The paper used in this publication meets the minimum requirements
of American National Standard for Information Sciences—Permanence
of Paper for Printed Library Materials, ANSI Z39.48-1984.

Distributed by
University of Hawai'i Press
2840 Kolowalu Street
Honolulu, Hawaii 96822

Cover design by Raymond Mun Kong Lum

CONTENTS

Foreword by Leigh-Wai Doo   vii
Foreword by Chun Chee-Kwon   ix
Preface   xi
Introduction   xv

1. Sun Yat-sen's Six Visits to Hawaii, 1879–1910
   The First Visit (June 1879–July 1883): Education in Honolulu   1
   The Second Visit (November 1884–April 1885):
       Settling Family Property Issue with Sun Mei   5
   The Third Visit (October 1894–January 1895):
       Founding the First Revolutionary Society in Hawaii   6
   The First Canton Uprising   10
   The Fourth Visit (January 1896–June 1896):
       Visiting Family and Friends, Preparing for Further Action   12
   Fateful Encounter with Dr. Cantlie   20
   The Fifth Visit (September 1903–March 1904): Reorganizing
       the Hsing Chung Hui and Founding the Revolutionary Army   21
   The Sixth Visit (March 1910–May 1910):
       Forming the Tung Meng Hui Hawaii Chapter   31
   Sun Returns to China   35
   The Mystery of Sun Yat-sen's Birth Certificate   39

2. Sun Yat-sen's Fund-Raising in Hawaii   42
   Hawaii's Contributions to the Ten Uprisings   42
   Funding the First Canton Uprising   43
   The Second Uprising   44
   The Third through the Eighth Uprisings 1907–1908   46
   The Ninth Uprising   46

The Tenth Uprising	47
First Military Bond Issued in Hawaii	47
Donations from the Broad Masses of the People	48
Four Letter to Hawaii Asking for Donations	50
Contributions of the Chinese in Hilo	52
The American Chinese Revolutionary Army Fund-Raising Bureau	55
Fund-Raising after the Establishment of the Republic	60
Accounting for the Funds Raised	62
Repayment of the Bonds	64
3. Sun Yat-sen's Supporters in Hawaii	67
Hsing Chung Hui Members Who Attended the First Meeting	68
Others Who Joined the Hsing Chung Hui After the First Meeting	74
Members of the Chung Hua Keming Jun in Hilo, 1903–1904	78
Members of the Tung Meng Hui in Hawaii, 1910–1912	81

Appendixes

I. Extracts from Punahou School Archives	93
II. Punahou Alumni Directory Information Card	95
III. Punahou School Ledger	96
IV. Members Who Attended the First Meeting of the Hsing Chung Hui	97
V. Hsing Chung Hui Members and Ledger of Dates and Payments of Membership Fees	98
VI. Members of the Chung Hua Keming Jun (Chinese Revolutionary Army)	101
VII. Members Who Joined the Tung Meng Hui in 1910	102
VIII. Members of the Tung Meng Hui, Hilo, 1910	103
IX. News Item from The Chinese People's Daily (Overseas Edition), August 26, 1985	104
X. Sun Yat-sen's Two Letters of Condolence to Hilo Comrades and Lai Hip's Family, December 14, 1915, and January 25, 1916	105
XI. News Item in the *Pacific Commercial Adviser,* October 7, 1903: "Noted Reformer Sun Arrives Here Quietly"	107
XII. News Item in the *Pacific Commercial Adviser,* December 14, 1903: "Dr. Sun Advocates A Revolt In China"	108
Notes	109
Glossary	117
Bibliography	121
Index	125

FOREWORD

by Leigh-wai Doo

The Dr. Sun Yat-sen Hawaii Foundation is pleased to have stimulated this English version of *Sun Yat-sen in Hawaii—Activities and Supporters*. An article was originally published in 1996 in Beijing, China, in Chinese with a circulation limited within China. This book, coauthored by Yansheng and Raymond Lum, significantly expands and revises the original work.

Sun Yat-sen in Hawaii—Activities and Supporters is one of the most comprehensive and detailed accounts available in English on Dr. Sun's life and revolutionary activities in Hawaii. It includes an extensive listing of many of his supporters in Hawaii a century ago, whose descendants today have prominent Hawaii family names such as Ai, Chang, Ching, Heen, Dang, Damon, Hee, Ho, Lau, Leong, Lee, Loo, Loui, Luke, Lum, Soong, Sun, Tam, Wong, Yap, Young, and Zane among thousand supporters.

The people in the Kingdom of Hawaii and later Territory of Hawaii, U.S.A., were principal contributors to Dr. Sun's early year education, moral values, and support of the Democratic Revolution of 1911, and the subsequent unification efforts of Dr. Sun in China. As Dr. Lin Jia You, director of the Dr. Sun Yat-sen Institute of Zhong Shan University in Guangzhou, China, has said, "Without his experience in Hawaii, there would not be the great career of Dr. Sun Yat-sen." It was in Hawaii that Dr. Sun Yat-sen developed the concepts and the moral character that were the foundations of his career. As a boy of thirteen, Sun Tai Chu learned English with such a proficiency that four years later he received an award from King Kalakaua of Hawaii. His concepts of government evolved from his schooling, which exposed him to the British and American systems of democracy. His character evolved, in those formative years of thirteen to seventeen years old, from the Anglican Iolani School and the Protestant Punahou School.

Manpower and funds came from Dr. Sun Yat-sen's brethren who had emigrated to Hawaii from Zhongshan County in China, where they spoke the same dialect and had common relatives and friends. It was with this group of Chinese in Hawaii that he formed the first revolutionary party of China, Hsing Chung Hui, in 1894 and took refuge after the first of many revolutionary attempts in China. From the people of Hawaii he raised funds, sold bonds, and gained volunteers to fight in China, including in the later years, stimulating China's first air force with funds and pilots from overseas Chinese. Dr. Sun Yat-sen came to Hawaii six times, living a total of seven years in Hawaii. His closeness to Hawaii and the confidence he felt in being a *kamaaina,* a person of the land of Hawaii, is reflected in his statement to a newspaper reporter in 1910: "This is my Hawaii. Here I was brought up and educated; and it was here that I came to know what modern, civilized governments are like and what they mean."

These and other documents and facts are the types of material being researched, organized, and chronicled by the Dr. Sun Yat-sen Hawaii Foundation. The Foundation's mission is to preserve and chronicle the activities of Dr. Sun Yat-sen and his supporters in Hawaii. Visit out Website *http://library.kcc.hawaii.edu/sun* and hear Dr. Sun Yat-sen's voice in person. Share with us your documents and knowledge.

We owe a great debt of gratitude to coauthors Yansheng and Raymond Lum, who volunteered to write this book, the University of Hawaii Press, and countless volunteers who are saving history. Appreciation is particularly extended to the Hawaii Chinese History Center for substantial contributions in funds and in efforts to preserve the history of Chinese in Hawaii which otherwise might have been lost with the passing of generations. *Sun Yat-sen in Hawaii—Activities and Supporters* is one of the fundamental works of both Hawaii's and China's history.

Leigh-wai Doo is the president of the Dr. Sun Yat-sen Hawaii Foundation. His great-grandfather, Young Ahin, was a follower and supporter of Dr. Sun. His grandfather, Yang Xian Yi, was born and reared in Hawaii and was also a follower of Dr. Sun. Yang Xian Yi went to China to work with Dr. Sun and died for the revolution. Dr. Sun called him the "Father of Aviation in China."

FOREWORD

by Chun Chee-kwon

Hawaii played a very important role in the life of Dr. Sun Yat-sen. Not only did he spend many years here, his family lived here from 1896 to 1908. Dr. Sun's only son, Sun Fo, came to Hawaii when he was four years old. Sun Fo grew up on his uncle Sun Mei's Kula ranch in Maui, and he studied at the St. Louis High School in Honolulu. As a young man, Sun Fo followed his father and participated in the revolutionary activities led by his father. In 1910, he worked as a translator for the *Chee Yow Shin Bo* (Liberty News), a Chinese newspaper sponsored by his father to publicize revolutionary ideas. When the Tung Meng Hui Hawaiian chapter was first formed in Honolulu in 1910, Sun Fo participated in the first meeting and became a member.

Sun Fo married Chun Shuk-ying, who happened to be my first cousin. Chun Shuk-ying was born and grew up in Honolulu. Soon she married Sun Fo, and they left Hawaii and went to Berkeley, California. After the Republic of China was established, they went back to live in China. In 1934, while Sun Fo was the president of the Legislative Yuan of the Chinese government in Nanking, he returned to Hawaii for a visit. It was then that I went to China with him and worked for him as his English secretary. I lived with the Sun family for many years. When I was in China during that period, I met many friends and relatives who knew Dr. Sun personally. I was not surprised to find that many of them were from Hawaii.

Over the years, I have collected many publications on Dr. Sun Yat-sen, from China and all over the world. I hoped to find more information about Dr. Sun's activities in Hawaii as well as stories of those Chinese in Hawaii who followed and supported him. I have been disappointed. Some information is lost and a lot is not fully documented. Today, those people who worked with Dr. Sun or who knew him personally have passed away and their descendants are also passing away. We are faced with the urgent task to preserve whatever information we can for the generations to come.

Then I heard that Raymond Lum and his wife Yansheng were doing research and writing a book on this subject. Raymond and I were schoolmates at the University of Hawaii in the 1930s and have been fraternity brothers ever since. Ray's father, Lum Chee, was a merchant in Hilo and a follower of Dr. Sun beginning in 1903, when Dr. Sun first visited Hilo. Ray told me stories he heard from his father that in those days, when Dr. Sun and his followers held meetings, they always had the blinds drawn. There was an atmosphere of secrecy surrounding the revolutionaries. It was absolutely necessary because the Manchu regime put a price on Dr. Sun's head and the Manchu consuls in Hawaii kept a close watch on Dr. Sun as well as those Chinese who supported him. In those days, people risked their lives and their family members' safety to support the revolution. This was one reason why people kept their activities a secret and destroyed papers that might incriminate them.

Fortunately, Lum Chee kept many letters, military bonds, and other memorabilia of the revolution in the safe of his store. Ray and Yansheng did painstaking research on these papers and put them into historical context. They have gone through available publications, including books, articles, and all kinds of material, both English and Chinese. They visited and identified historical sites where Dr. Sun's activities took place, and they talked to many family members and descendants of Dr. Sun's followers. Luckily, today in Hawaii, one can still find some people who, directly or indirectly, know something about this part of history.

The Lums also did painstaking research to put together short biographical sketches of some sixty Chinese in Hawaii who at one time or other followed and supported Dr. Sun. I think this is very good. We should not forget our ancestors who sometimes put their lives at risk in supporting the revolution while many others gave generous donations to support the armed uprisings against the Manchu regime. Of course, what has been recorded in this book is far from complete. There were many unsung heroes whose names and activities were not included. We can only hope that his book will stimulate more research on this subject.

The Lums are to be complimented for a job well done. As many materials on the activities of Dr. Sun and his supporters in Hawaii have been published in Chinese and have not been translated into English, this book will make this information accessible to the English-reading public. I believe this book will help readers get a more complete picture of the life of the great revolutionary, Dr. Sun Yat-sen, in Hawaii and the historic role Hawaii played in the birth of modern China.

PREFACE

Raymond Lum's father, Lum Chee, was a follower of Dr. Sun Yat-sen from 1903. He kept a collection of Dr. Sun Yat-sen's letters, one signed and written in Dr. Sun's own handwriting; a canceled check endorsed by Dr. Sun; and military bonds and other memorabilia of the revolution. Lum Chee told Ray to donate his collection to China one day. After the normalization of Sino-American relations in 1978, Raymond started looking for someone who could help him find the right person or institute in China to whom he could donate his father's collection.

The process was not smooth sailing. There were many twists and turns, and luckily, everything turned out well and ended in a romance.

In 1979, Ray met Chun Chee-kwon in Hong Kong. Since Chee-kwon is related to the Sun family, he knows Soong Ching Ling (Madame Sun Yat-sen) well. Chee-kwon was on his way to visit Beijing and planned to go together with Ray so that he could introduce Ray to Madame Soong Ching Ling, to whom Ray could donate Lum Chee's collection. Unfortunately, just before they were leaving for China, Chee-kwon's son was killed in a plane crash in Chicago, and he had to cancel his trip to China. The following year, more unfortunate news came: Madame Soong Ching Ling had passed away.

Ray continued to try other channels, and by coincidence, his close friend Mac Kramer was visiting China with a group of members from the U.S. Committee for UNICEF in 1980 and Ma Yansheng happened to be the representative of the All China Women's Federation to guide them around. A few years later, Kramer introduced Ma Yansheng to Ray and asked Yansheng to help find the right person or institute to receive the historical documents. Finally, in 1985, a meeting was arranged with the Sun Yat-sen Society in Beijing, to which Ray donated the originals of the Lum Chee collection. Soon after, Ray's wife died. Ray and Yansheng were married in 1986.

Yansheng settled in Honolulu and started research on the history of Hawaii, especially the history of the Chinese in Hawaii. Naturally, Dr. Sun Yat-sen's revolutionary activities in Hawaii constituted an important part of the history. Yansheng wrote an article, "The Support of Overseas Chinese in Hawaii to the early Revolutionary Activities of Dr. Sun Yat-sen," which was published in the Chinese magazine *Overseas Chinese History Studies,* No. 4 (1996), in Beijing.

Then in 1997, the Dr. Sun Yat-sen Hawaii Foundation was formed in Honolulu. It was interested in the article and decided that it should be published in English so that the English-reading public would have access to these fascinating historical facts. This is how this book came about.

This book focuses on Dr. Sun's activities and his followers in Hawaii. It is not our intent to cover Sun's whole life and activities all over the world. The time frame of this book basically is from 1879, when Dr. Sun first came to Hawaii, to 1910, when he made his last visit to Hawaii. However, one or two relevant events in 1912 and 1915 are also included.

In the process of doing the research, we tried to put the letters, military bonds, and other memorabilia that Ray's father, Lum Chee, kept all these years in historical context. Each paper had a story to tell: for example, when it was issued, how and by whom, who bought the bonds, how much money was raised, and how the funds were used. These papers come alive.

Then we identified the historical sites where Dr. Sun's activities were staged. This included the school campuses where Dr. Sun studied; Dr. Sun's former residence, Sun Mei's Kula ranch on Maui; the first meeting place of the Hsing Chung Hui and the Tung Meng Hui in Honolulu; the site in Honolulu's Chinatown where Dr. Sun made speeches to hundreds of people; and so forth. Unfortunately, most of the old buildings have been demolished. However, pictures of the sites where these historical events took place are included here.

A lot of information has been published in articles and books written by historians and writers who did research and preserved precious records of this part of history. The works on which we have depended most heavily are listed in the bibliography.

We would like to express our special thanks to the publishers of *The Pictorial History of the Republic of China* (Taipei, 1978) for granting permission to copy some photographs from the book and of *Manuscripts of the Founding Father* (Taipei, 1961) for permission to copy one of Sun Yat-sen's letters. We have also drawn on the following pictorial books: *Historical Traces of Sun Yat-sen's Activities in Hong Kong, Macao and Overseas* (Hong Kong, 1986); *Sun Zhong-shan,* published by the Shanghai Museum of Sun Yat-sen's Former Residence (1996); and *Pictorial of Mr. Sun Zhong-shan,* published by the Museum of the Chinese Revolution, Beijing (1986).

Our thanks and acknowledgements to the following organizations and individuals: The Hawaii Chinese History Center; its president, Roger Liu, and all the board members; and its former president, Puanani Woo, and her husband, Francis Woo. The publication of this book was underwritten by the Hawaii Chinese History Center. Part of the cost of publication was also underwritten by the Dr. Sun Yat-sen Hawaii Foundation.

We would like to thank Bill Ching and the Ket On Society; Tom Yee and the See Dai Doo Society; Chun Chee-kwon and Wong Sau-chen, who kindly lent us their collections of books and publications on Sun Yat-sen and who also provided precious information, and their daughter Yan Chun, who helped in many ways to make the publication of this work possible; Susan Campbell of the Iolani School Archives; Mary Judd of the Punahou School Archives; Marilyn Reppur of the Hawaiian Mission Children's Society Library; and the Hawaii State Archives.

Thanks to those whom we interviewed: Young Wah-duck, Leigh-wai Doo, C. F. Damon, Jr., Carolyn Luke, K. Russell Ho, Ching Ping-quon, Owen Loui, Frank Eng, Pang Hong-kwun, Loo Ngan-sum, Henry Lau, Bill Tavares, Emma Rose Tavares, Ernest Loo, Richard Lum, Frank Lee, Mr. and Mrs. Eugene Yap, Veronica Meideros, Peter Baldwin, Loretta Pang, Lum Wing-tek, Elizabeth Lai Hip Lum, Ted Lum, Muriel Lai Hip De Ponte, Walter Watson, and Adrienne Chang Yee.

Special thanks to Bing Fai Lau, who helped with the translation of Chinese names; Calvin Mekaru of K&E Graphics for his patience and skill in reproducing negatives and art work; and Mamo Yokoyama of Associated Printers for his help in producing press proofs for the cover design. Special thanks to Michael E. Mcmillan for editing.

INTRODUCTION

Sun Yat-Sen (Sun Wen), the father of modern China, is one of the most honored and revered statesmen in the world. At the turn of the twentieth century, he led the Chinese people in a revolutionary movement that succeeded in overthrowing the Manchu dynasty, thus ending more than two thousand years of imperial rule in China. In October 1911, a republic was established, and he was elected the first provisional president. The Republic of China was also the first republic ever to be established in Asia.

Hawaii and its people played an important role in the life of Sun. Hawaii was known as Sun's second home for he spent his teenage years here. He had family and many friends in these islands, where he carried out important revolutionary activities. During his years in exile outside of China, he was not allowed to land in many countries, for example, the Dutch Indies (now Indonesia). Even in Japan, where he spent many years, using it as a base for his activities, he occasionally found himself not so welcomed. But he never had any difficulties in returning to the Islands. The Hawaiians, especially those of Chinese ancestry, wholeheartedly supported him financially and politically. In many instances, they risked their lives to support the revolution. Sun once said: "Hua Qiao [overseas Chinese] is the mother of the revolution." The Chinese in Hawaii are well worthy of such an honor.

Hawaii played a historic role in the birth of modern China. It was known as the cradle of the Chinese revolution because it was here in the Islands that Sun founded the first revolutionary organization, the Hsing Chung Hui (Revive China Society) 興中會, which later developed into a strong political party called the Tung Meng Hui (Alliance Society) 同盟會, which overthrew the Manchu regime. It was reorganized in 1912 to become the Kuomintang (Nationalist Party) 國民黨. It was in Hawaii that Sun and a little more than a hundred Chinese first vowed to bring down the Manchus, and this little spark ignited into a prairie fire that burned down the decaying Manchu regime.

ONE

Sun Yat-sen's Six Visits to Hawaii, 1879–1910

THE FIRST VISIT (JUNE 1879–JULY 1883): EDUCATION IN HONOLULU

Sun Yat-sen was born on November 12, 1866, in Choy Hang village, Chung Shan District, Kwangtung Province. He first came to Hawaii in 1879, when he was thirteen years old.[1] During his lifetime, he made six trips to the Islands. His cumulative time in Hawaii amounted to more than seven years.

Sun was able to come to Hawaii because of his brother, Sun Mei, who was locally known as S. Ahmi. Sun Mei's uncle, Young Mun-nap (Sun Mei's mother's brother), came to Hawaii earlier and was a quite successful merchant in Honolulu. In 1871, Sun Mei left his impoverished home village and came to the Islands with his uncle to start a new life. He began as a vegetable farmer and later was a rice planter in Ewa, Oahu. He saved some money, opened a store, and was involved in recruiting Chinese contract laborers to come to Hawaii to work on the sugar plantations. His success and prosperity gave Sun Yat-sen the opportunity to come to Hawaii to study.

When young Sun first came, he worked in his brother's store in Ewa for a few months. In September 1879, he enrolled in Iolani School and was graduated in the summer of 1882. At that time, Iolani was run by the Anglican Church and was one of the best schools in Honolulu. In Iolani School, Sun used the name Tai Cheong 帝象.[2] His name was spelled in many different ways, for example, Tai Chu at Punahou School (see Appendix 1) and Tai Chock in the 1841–1861 Punahou Alumni Directory (see Appendix 2).

When Sun studied at Iolani School, most of the students were Hawaiians or part-Hawaiians, and there were only a few Chinese students. Because he did not know a word of English, his teacher, Solomon Meheula, asked him to sit in the class as an observer for ten days. Then he was taught the alphabet, spelling, and grammar. Being a bright student, he learned quite rapidly. When he graduated in 1882, he was second in grammar and was awarded a prize by King Kalakaua at a ceremony. In attendance were the dowager Queen Emma and Princess Liliuokalani. The Chinese community was very proud of this event.

FIGURE. 1.1. The Iolani School campus from 1872 to 1902. Sun studied on this campus, located at Bates Street and Nuuanu Street. Iolani School has since moved many times, and this campus was demolished long ago. Photo courtesy of the Archives of Iolani School.

FIGURE 1.2. The Bates-Nuuanu intersection as it appeared in 1998. The old school campus was located on the right side of the road. Homes now occupy the site. Photo by Yansheng Ma Lum.

When Sun was in school, he combed his hair into a queue like all Chinese in those days. Some of the boys would tease him and pull his queue for fun. When the younger or weaker boys did that, Sun would tolerate them. But he fought against those who were older and taught them a lesson so that they would not insult him again. This story shows that even in his younger days, Sun would help the weak and resist bullies.[3]

There are different versions of where and for how long Sun studied after he graduated from Iolani. For example, some say he studied at St. Louis High School. How-

FIGURE. 1.3. Iolani School in 1998. Photo by Yansheng Ma Lum.

ever, no record could be found of Sun's presence at St. Louis. The Punahou School archives confirms that Sun entered Punahou in the spring of 1883. In the 1882–1883 catalog of Punahou School (then called Oahu College), Sun was listed under the name of Tai Chu. In the Punahou School archives, there is also a ledger that recorded the payment of $55.00 to the account of Tai Chu, dated June 19, 1883 (Appendix 3).

At Punahou School, Sun was taught by Francis W. Damon, who was very much impressed by young Sun's intellect and charisma. A close friendship ensued, and in later years Damon remained one of Sun's good friends and staunch supporters.

Sun studied one semester at Punahou and would have liked to pursue his studies in Hawaii and later in the United States, but Sun Mei felt that his brother had had enough education. To make matters worse, young Sun expressed his wish to become a Christian. Sun Mei was shocked that his brother would betray Chinese culture for a foreign religion. He wrote to their father, and orders came to send young Sun back to China immediately. In July 1883, Sun Yat-sen returned to his home village.

However, these early years had an important influence on Sun's life. He once said that his ideas came from three main sources: Chinese traditional culture, Western ideas, and his own thoughts; but Western ideas prevailed.[4] In his handwritten autobiography of 1896, he described his first voyage to Hawaii on board the SS *Grannock:* "I saw the wonderful steamship and the vast ocean . . . and deep in my heart, I wished to learn from the West and seek for the infinite truth."[5]

During his years at Iolani and Punahou, he was exposed to Western culture, was strongly influenced by it, and in his young mind, the seeds of Western democracy were planted.

FIGURE 1.4. The gate of Punahou School, with the old school logo, on Punahou Street, Honolulu. Photographed in 1998 by Yansheng Ma Lum.

FIGURE 1.5. The old school house of Punahou School, built in 1852. Sun Yat-sen attended classes in this building. Photographed in 1998 by Yansheng Ma Lum.

FIGURE. 1.6. Sun Yat-sen in an 1883 photograph. Reproduced from *Sun Yat-sen* (Shanghai: Shanghai Museum of Sun Yat-sen's Former Residence, 1996).

In an interview in 1910, Sun told Albert Pierce Taylor, a newspaperman and later a librarian in the State Archives of Hawaii: "This is *my* Hawaii . . . here I was brought up and educated; and it was here that I came to know what modern, civilized governments are like and what they mean."[6]

Sun admired Hawaii, and on one occasion he said that although Hawaii was a small island kingdom, it had law and order, and the people were happy and prosperous. He said that if China was not revived, although there were 400 million people, the Chinese could not even keep up with the Hawaiians.[7]

THE SECOND VISIT (NOVEMBER 1884–APRIL 1885): SETTLING FAMILY PROPERTY ISSUE WITH SUN MEI

Back in his home village, young Sun Yat-sen got into trouble. One day when he and his good friend Lu How-tung went to the village temple, he broke the arm of a wooden idol trying to show to the superstitious villagers that the idol was powerless. This caused a big commotion, and he was forced to leave home and go to Hong Kong, where he continued to study English in a school called the Diocesan Home. There, he met the Rev. Charles B. Hager of the American Congregational Mission, and in the winter of 1883 he was baptized.[8]

When Sun Mei heard of the outrageous acts that his brother had committed, he thought he had better step in to discipline the young man. He sent for him to return to Hawaii. So in November 1884, Sun Yat-sen arrived in Maui. In 1881, Sun Mei had moved to Kahului, Maui. He first opened a store and later leased land from the government and developed a 3,900-acre cattle ranch, which was located at a small town called Keokea in the Kula area.

Sun Mei was very angry at his brother and reprimanded him harshly, saying that he should strictly abide by Chinese tradition and refrain from doing things that would bring trouble and misfortune to the whole family. Hoping that his brother would work together with him to develop a family business, Sun Mei had registered half of his property in Sun Yat-sen's name. Realizing now that his brother had no desire to become a businessman, Sun Mei requested the return of Sun's share of the property. Sun Yat-sen willingly agreed and planned to go back to China. Sun Mei did not give him any money for the return passage, thinking this might pressure his brother to change his mind, but to no avail.

Sun Yat-sen was determined and left Maui for Honolulu penniless. His friend Francis W. Damon helped him raise $300. His classmate C. K. Ai helped him with five dollars, which was then Ai's salary for one month in a tailor shop. From his shop, he provided Sun some clothing as well.[9]

Later, Sun Mei regretted that he was too harsh with his brother and sought reconciliation. Sun Mei financed his brother's education in the medical schools of Canton and Hong Kong. Sun graduated at the top of his class in the College of Medicine in Hong Kong, and in 1893 and 1894, he practiced medicine in Macao and Canton. He was very successful as a doctor, and his clinic was crowded with patients requesting his services.

In the meantime, China was in turmoil. Foreign powers encroached on the ancient empire. The Manchu government, conservative and corrupt, was defeated and humiliated time and again. Unequal treaties were signed, ceding sovereignty, treaty ports, and enormous indemnities. China was in danger of being carved up by foreign powers. Progressive-minded people began to awaken, and a revolutionary tide to modernize China, with Sun at the forefront, was surging forward. In 1883, war broke out between China and France in the southern part of China. The Chinese army won a big victory at Zhen-nan-guan, where the French army was almost completely routed. Then the most incredible thing happened. The Manchu regime, whose army had won the war, sued for peace with France and signed an unequal treaty ceding Indochina to the French. It was an unprecedented incident, and it fully exposed the stupidity of the Manchu regime. Sun said in his autobiography narrating the history of the ten uprisings that it was after this war that he lost all hope in the Manchu regime and made up his mind to overthrow the dynasty and establish a republic.[10]

THE THIRD VISIT (OCTOBER 1894–JANUARY 1895): FOUNDING THE FIRST REVOLUTIONARY SOCIETY IN HAWAII

In 1894, the Manchu regime was again defeated by Japan. The whole country rose up in protest and lost all hope. Sun thought this was the time to act, and he decided to go abroad to raise funds from the overseas Chinese and organize armed uprisings against the Manchu regime. The first place he went was Hawaii, where he arrived in October 1894. In Honolulu, he rallied a small group of friends and relatives and founded the Hsing Chung Hui (Revive China Society). This was the

FIGURE. I.7. Ho Fon's house on Emma Lane. Photo courtesy of *The Pictorial History of the Republic of China* (Taipei, 1978).

first revolutionary organization that Sun formed, and its founding was an important milestone in the history of modern China. It was a first step toward overthrowing the Manchu dynasty and a clarion call to the Chinese people to rise up, free themselves from Manchu rule, and build a strong and democratic China.

On November 24, 1894, a meeting was held at the home of Ho Fon, which was located at Emma Lane, Honolulu. Ho Fon, Sun's good friend, was a leader in the First Chinese Church of Christ and worked at the Bank of Bishop and Co., Ltd., in Honolulu. At the meeting, it was decided that a revolutionary society should be formed. Because Ho Fon's home was not big enough, the participants gathered in Lee Chong's home, which was also situated on Emma Lane. An initiation ceremony was held where some twenty-odd people attended. Participants took an oath to "drive away the Tartars, recover China for the Chinese, and establish a republic." They also swore allegiance to keep faith with the society and its doctrine and to work for the cause at all times.

At the meeting, Sun was the first one to be sworn in, placing his hand on the Bible and quietly asking God to witness his oath. The others quickly followed suit.[11] (The names of the participants are listed in Appendix 4.)

At the meeting, Lau Cheong (owner of the Wing Wo Tai store in Honolulu), was elected president and Ho Fon, vice-president. In the following months, more than a hundred members joined. It was decided that members should pay a membership fee of five dollars. Ho Fon kept a ledger of members and dates and payments of membership fees for thirty years. This precious record provides important facts about this great event. The names of the more than a hundred people who joined and paid membership fees were recorded in the ledger. It was published in *The Chinese of Hawaii* (Honolulu, 1929; see Appendix 5).

FIGURE 1.8. Lee Chong's house on Emma Lane. Photo courtesy of *The Pictorial History of the Republic of China* (Taipei, 1978).

FIGURE 1.9. Emma Lane, Honolulu. The old houses of Ho Fon and Lee Chong have been demolished, and a parking lot stands where the two houses used to be. Photograph taken in 1998 by Yansheng Ma Lum.

After the Hsing Chung Hui was established in Honolulu, Lee Chong and Soong Kee-yun secretly went to Kula, Maui, to persuade Sun Mei to join. Sun Mei gladly joined and took on the chairmanship of the Kahului branch. He persuaded Dang Yum-nam to join, and Dang became the chairman of the Paia branch. Dang alone brought fifteen more members to join.[12]

FIGURE 1.10. A statue of Sun Yat-sen holding the declaration of the Hsing Chung Hui stands at the Sun Yat-sen Mall in Honolulu's Chinatown. The statue was donated by the people of Kaohsiung, Taiwan, in 1984 on the ninetieth anniversary of the Hsing Chung Hui. Photo by Yansheng Ma Lum.

When the Hsing Chung Hui was founded, Sun had the support of only a small group of people. At that time, most people were working hard to make a living and knew little about the revolution. Moreover, it would be risky to be involved in trying to overthrow the Manchu regime as their family members in China might be persecuted. Often, when Sun was walking on the streets of Honolulu's Chinatown, people would point at his back and call him "the crazy fellow who wanted to overthrow the emperor."[13]

In his autobiography narrating the history of the ten uprisings before the founding of the Republic of China, Sun wrote:

> I worked in Hawaii for a few months, talking about the revolution. But people were not interested, only a few people responded. My friend Dang Yum-nam and my brother Sun Mei gave all they could to help. There were only scores of other relatives and friends who helped me.[14]

From 1894 to 1895, 120-130 Chinese in Hawaii joined the Hsing Chung Hui.[15] Most of the members were small merchants, workers, and intellectuals. In Honolulu, there was a Chinese-English Debating Society, which was formed by a group of intellectuals in 1883. The best-known among them were Lee Chong, Sun's childhood friend Luke Chan, and well-known merchant Yap Kwai-fong. Sun Yat-sen was asked to be their honorary president, and most of the members of the society joined the Hsing Chung Hui.[16]

FIGURE I.II. The Hsing Chung Hui Memorial Hall at Sun Yat-sen Mall in Honolulu was inaugurated in 1984. Photo by Yansheng Ma Lum.

To raise funds for the revolution, members paid membership fees and Sun issued Hsing Chung Hui bonds. It was promised that the buyers would be repaid tenfold after the revolution succeeded. The Hsing Chung Hui ledger recorded those who bought the bonds. Athough Sun was able to raise only $1,380, this was a considerable sum at that time, and it was also the first sum raised by Sun to start the revolution.

In the meantime, Hsing Chung Hui members in Honolulu started military training. They wanted to prepare themselves to go back to China to join armed uprisings. The playground of Mills School (today's Mid-Pacific Institute) was turned over to them by Francis W. Damon as a drilling field. In his autobiography, *My Seventy Nine Years in Hawaii,* C. K. Ai wrote: "There were over forty of us when we started the training, but because our Danish drill-master was very strict, the boys simply faded away and it was not long before we didn't have enough volunteers to continue."[17]

THE FIRST CANTON UPRISING

Sun left Hawaii in January 1895 and returned to China to instigate an uprising. Following him back home were Dang Yum-nam, Soong Kee-yun, How Ai-chin (a tailor), Ha Park-chee, Ching Nam (a cook), and Lee Kai (a worker). They were all Hsing Chung Hui members.[18]

Soong Kee-yun owned a little restaurant where Sun used to go for his meals. They discussed the need for revolution in China and became good friends. Soong sold his business and went back to China and joined in many revolutionary activities. Soong married a part-Hawaiian woman and had two part-Hawaiian sons whom he took back to China. Both sons died for the revolution.[19] Dang Yumnam liquidated his personal assets, donated a large sum of money, and followed Sun back to China to participate in the revolution.

Sun went to Hong Kong and there the Hsing Chung Hui headquarters was founded. At the first meeting, members unanimously agreed to take action and launch an armed uprising. Sun left for Canton and, together with his childhood friend Lu How-tung and others, began to make plans. Unfortunately, news of their planning leaked out, and the Manchu regime arrested some of the participants. Lu How-tung and other leaders were caught and beheaded. Sun narrowly escaped to Hong Kong and then to Japan.

This started his more than sixteen years of exile during which he traveled all over the United States, Canada, Europe, Japan, and Southeast Asia to rally the overseas Chinese and the people of the world to support the revolution. The Manchu regime put a price of one thousand silver dollars on his head and ordered its ambassadors in Hong Kong, Tokyo, the United States, and Europe to spy on Sun and to bring him back to China for execution.

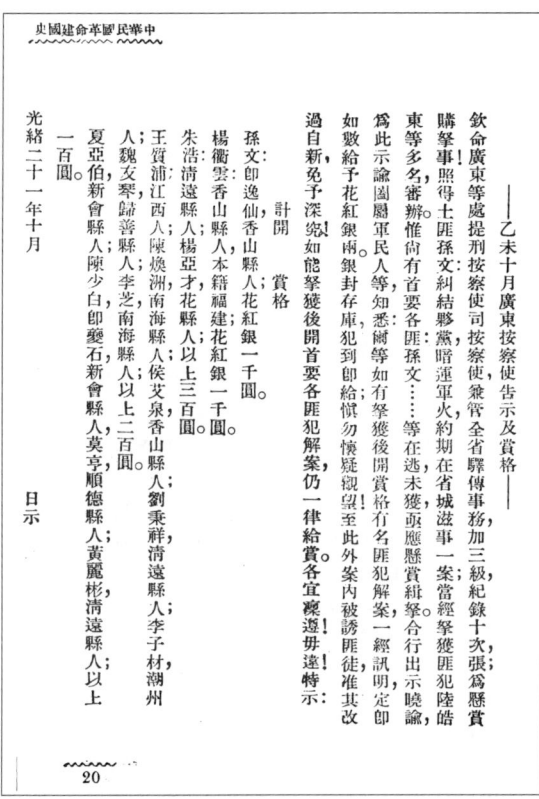

FIGURE 1.12. The "wanted" poster put up by the administration of Kwangtung Province. Reproduced from *The Revolutionary History of the Founding of the Republic of China* (1929).

The "Wanted" poster put up by the administration of Kwangtung Province reads in part:

> ... Bandit Sun Wen gathered a group of people and smuggled guns and ammunition, trying to cause disturbances ... and to escape from town. ... Whoever informs on the listed fugitives will be awarded as promised. ...
>
> Awards for apprehending the following bandits:
> Sun Wen: also named Yat-sen, native of Heungshan, one thousand silver dollars. ...
> How Ai-chin, native of Heungshan, ... the above people, two hundred silver dollars each. ...
> Ha Ah-park, native of Hsinghui, ... the above people, one hundred silver dollars each. ...
>
> Date: October 1895.

Among the listed fugitives are How Ai-chin and Ha Ah-park (Ha Park-chee). They were both from Hawaii and followed Sun back to China.[20]

This incident is known as the First Canton Uprising. It was the first ever to be staged against the Manchu regime and was followed by nine others, all of which failed. Finally, the Wuchang Uprising, staged on October 10, 1911, succeeded in toppling the Manchu regime and establishing the Republic of China.

THE FOURTH VISIT (JANUARY 1896–JUNE 1896): VISITING FAMILY AND FRIENDS, PREPARING FOR FURTHER ACTION

Shortly after the failure of the First Canton Uprising, in early 1896, Sun came to Hawaii from Japan. At that time, his good friend Luke Chan had gone back to China to get married. As Luke was returning to Hawaii, Sun asked him to bring Sun's family to Hawaii because it would not be safe for them to stay in China. Luke Chan came back to Hawaii together with Sun's mother; Sun's first wife, Loo Mu-chun; their five-year-old son, Sun Fo; and a baby daughter, Sun Yuen. They arrived safely at Maui and lived at Sun Mei's Kula ranch. When Sun Yat-sen came to Hawaii in 1896, he stayed at the Kula ranch, which became known as the former residence of Sun Yat-sen in Hawaii.

Sun was happy to spend some time with his family. He told Sun Mei about the failure of the First Canton Uprising. Sun Mei, who had became a staunch supporter of the revolution, encouraged his brother to continue the struggle.[21]

When Sun was in Hawaii, he had the reputation of being a good doctor, and many friends and relatives came to him for medical services. Harriet (Pak Hoy) Wong of Wailuku, Maui, who lived to be one hundred years old and died a few years ago, told a story about the smallpox vaccination she got from Sun. There was a scar on her arm, a result of the vaccination Sun administered with a bamboo needle. He charged the boys two dollars and the girls one dollar. Mrs. Wong asked why he charged her less. Sun replied: "Because you are a girl." Mrs. Wong disliked the differential treatment given to males and females. This became a well-known story among the Chinese in Maui.[22]

FIGURE 1.13. This family picture taken in Hawaii in 1903 was later published in the Honolulu *Sunday Advertiser,* January 7, 1912. In the center is Sun's mother, Elderly Lady Young. The girl in front of her is Sun's second daughter, Sun On. On her left is Sun's first daughter, Sun Yuen, and on her right is Sun's son, Sun Fo. Back row, left to right: a maid; Tom Shee, Sun Mei's wife; nephew Si Wei; Sun Mei; Sun Yat-sen; Loo Mu-chun, Sun Yat-sen's wife; Sun Xia, an adopted daughter; another maid. They lived at the Kula ranch until 1907. Photo reproduced from *Sun Yat-sen* (Shanghai: Shanghai Museum of Sun Yat-sen's Former Residence, 1996).

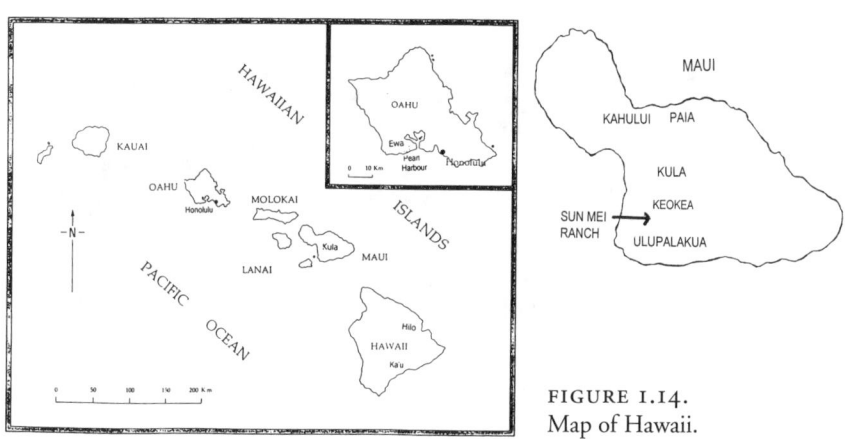

FIGURE 1.14. Map of Hawaii.

FIGURE 1.15. Front view of the buildings at Sun Mei's Kula ranch. Photo courtesy of the Hawaii Chinese History Center.

FIGURE 1.16. Rear view of the buildings at Sun Mei's Kula ranch. Photo courtesy of the Hawaii Chinese History Center.

FIGURE 1.17. Sun Mei's ranch site photographed in 1998. The big banyan tree in the picture is the same tree seen next to the ranch buildings in fig. 1.16. The level ground to the right of the tree is where the original buildings used to be. Photo by Henry Lau.

FIGURE 1.18. Remnant rocks of the old wall of Sun Mei's Kula ranch photographed in 1998. Photo by Yansheng Ma Lum.

There is another story about a family discussion regarding Sun's abandoning his medical career to become a revolutionist. Sun's mother did not want to see Sun risking his life as a revolutionary. If Sun wanted to help people, she said, he could do so as a doctor. Why risk his life and lead the hectic existence of a revolutionary? Sun replied: "If I am a doctor, I can hope to cure one patient at a time. If I help China to free herself, I can help 400 million people." Sun Mei agreed with his brother, and so ended the discussion.[23]

Sun Mei supported the revolution and gave all he had. In 1906, he had practically exhausted his cash and had to file for bankruptcy. He returned to China, leaving behind his wife, who signed the papers to sell the Kula ranch to Antone Tavares in 1908. Tavares married Julia Akana, the daughter of Tang Kan. The Hawaiians called him "Akana Liili," which meant "Akana, the small man." Tang Kan was a wealthy merchant in Kula and a friend of Sun Mei. After Tavares bought the ranch, Tang Kan continued to work on the ranch for a while until the Haleakala Ranch Company bought the property in 1928.[24] Now the property is used by the company to raise cattle. The old ranch buildings are all gone. Only some rocks from the old ranch wall and an old banyan tree that used to grow next to the old buildings are there to remind people that the Sun family once lived here.

Today, one can visit Sun Mei's Kula ranch site by driving along the Kula highway to the little town called Keokea. In May 1998, we (the authors) visited the Sun Mei Kula ranch site. We drove on the Kula highway for miles and miles and found ourselves traveling in a vast and sparsely populated area. We could not but wonder how, almost a hundred years ago, Sun Mei, his family, and Sun Yat-sen came to such a faraway place. Today, we can drive in a four-wheel-drive truck. How did they travel such long distances a hundred years ago? We thought of the pioneer Chinese families that lived there. They traveled by riding horses or mules or sometimes walked.

We were told to look for the "Fong Store and the Ching Store" on the roadside. That was the site of the little town of Keokea. There the road forked. We took the road going in the direction of Ulupalakua. Before we arrived at Sun Mei's Kula ranch site, we came to the Sun Yat-sen Memorial Park, which was by the highway. It was built and inaugurated in 1989 by the Maui Hua Ren 200 Committee of the Governor's Commission Commemorating the Chinese Bicentennial. In 1995, the park was turned over to Maui County. The land for the park was donated by the Baldwin family, who owns the Haleakala Ranch Company. The president of the company is Peter Baldwin, who kindly granted permission for us to visit the old ranch site. In the garden, there is a Sun Yat-sen statue, facing and overlooking Sun Mei's Kula ranch site. The statue was donated by the people and government of Taiwan. In the garden were two huge stone lions, donated by Ping Tung County of Taiwan, Maui's sister county.

We left the garden and drove along further until we came to a narrow unpaved road. We turned and drove along the dirt road. Our guide told us we were riding

FIGURE 1.19. Sun Yat-sen statue in Kula Memorial Park, photographed in 1998. Photo by Yansheng Ma Lum.

FIGURE 1.20. Stone lion in Kula Memorial Park, photographed in 1998. Photo by Yansheng Ma Lum.

on the same road that Sun Yat-sen once followed, riding a horse or mule, when he came to his brother's ranch. This narrow dirt road was the original one leading to the ranch and had never been changed. We all fell silent, and in our hearts, we paid our respects to the great man who around a hundred years ago traveled on this same road. We also felt how lucky we were to be able to ride on the same road he once traveled.

Approximately eighty Chinese families with a total of some seven hundred people lived in Kula between 1880 and 1910. They formed a thriving community. Most of them were engaged in agriculture. Some grew vegetables and brought their produce to sell in Makawao or took it as far as Kahului, where the produce was then shipped to Honolulu. These early pioneer Chinese families prospered by working the land leased from the government and this area was developed through their hard work.[25]

When Sun Mei first came to Hawaii in 1871, he and Chang Keong came together, and the two later became business partners. In 1878, Chang Keong went back to China to get married. The following year, 1879, Chang chartered the ship SS *Grannock,* docking at Macao, to bring more Chinese immigrants to Hawaii. Sun Yat-sen came on the same ship together with Chang Keong and his wife. This is confirmed in Paul Linebarger's book, *Sun Yat Sen and the Chinese Republic:*

> Sun Mei's partner obtained the English steamship *Grannock,* which had been put under the co-partnership management, and the emigrant excursion was finally assembled. The SS *Grannock* was to sail from the harbor of Macao. (Sun) Wen renewed his campaign to go with the ship. . . . He would be with friends on the voyage, and his brother would be there at Honolulu to greet him.[26]

According to Sun's cousin, Sun Duan, who lived in China, Sun Mei's partner who chartered the ship was Chang Keong.[27] In Sun Yat-sen's handwritten autobiography of 1896, however, Sun said he came to Hawaii with his mother, and his mother returned to China the same year while he stayed on.[28] Most probably, Sun Yat-sen, his mother, Chang Keong, and Chang's wife all came to Hawaii on the SS *Grannock.*

Chang Keong had six daughters and many grandchildren. We talked with two of the granddaughters, Pang Hong-kwun and Loo Ngan-sum. They said their grandfather and Sun Mei were business partners. Hong-kwun said that after their grandfather died, their family went to live close to the ranch with the Sun family. Hong-kwun's mother was Chang Keong's fourth daughter. She was a close friend of Sun's first wife, Loo Mu-chun. Hong-kwun said her mother liked to tell them stories of the Sun family, but at that time, they did not pay too much attention. Her mother would say: "One day you people will regret that you did not listen to my stories carefully because these stories will become history." Sure enough, Hong-kwun said she regretted not paying enough attention to her mother's stories. In the 1910s and 1920s, the Chinese families gradually moved away from Kula. Hong-kwun's family moved to Honolulu, as most other families did.[29]

FIGURE 1.21. Chinese-style rosewood settee from Sun Mei's Kula ranch. Photo courtesy of William Tavares.

Loo Ngan-sum, whose mother was Chang Keong's second daughter, told the story that in 1972, when she visited the Sun Yat-sen Memorial Hall in Choy Hang village, she heard a tape recording that the Memorial Hall played for her. It said that when young Sun Yat-sen came to Hawaii, Mrs. Chang Keong, Ngan-sum's grandmother, came with him. During the voyage, Mrs. Chang was seasick and young Sun did a lot to help her. Ngan-sum said that when the Choy Hang Memorial Hall staff members learned that she was Chang Keong's granddaughter, they invited her to lunch and treated her like a VIP. Ngan-sum also said that after Sun Yat-sen was elected president of the Republic of China, people told her grandmother the news and her grandmother was so surprised that she could not believe it. She exclaimed: "Ah, that young boy?"[30]

William Tavares, son of Antone Tavares, who bought Sun Mei's ranch, kept some of the artifacts from the ranch, an old Chinese rosewood settee and a Japanese samurai sword. A few years ago, he retired from his job as the principal of Makawao Elementary School. He said these artifacts were very precious to him and he wanted to keep them in the family. He told his children that in case there was a fire, the first thing to save were the settee and the sword. He also said that he was not going to sell the artifacts to anybody, but one day he might give them away—to China, if one day Taiwan and China are united.[31]

In 1896, when Sun went back to the Kula ranch to visit with his family, he did not stay long. He returned to Honolulu to work with the Hsing Chung Hui members. After the First Canton Uprising failed, some followers were disappointed, but the members of the Chinese-English Debating Society were there to welcome Sun when he came back to Honolulu and invited him to speak to them. Sun made a report on the situation in China and his ideas about the revolution. The members of the society were most enthusiastic, and they were among those who made the most donations to the revolution.[32]

FIGURE 1.22. Japanese samurai sword from Sun Mei's Kula ranch, photographed in 1998. Photo courtesy of William Tavares.

FATEFUL ENCOUNTER WITH DR. CANTLIE

As fate would have it, Hawaii, at the crossroads of the Pacific, played another special role in the life of Sun. One day during Sun's visit to Honolulu in 1896, as he was walking on the streets, he ran into Dr. James Cantlie, the dean of the College of Medicine in Hong Kong and his teacher and good friend. When Sun was practicing medicine in Hong Kong, whenever he needed advice on important surgeries, Dr. Cantlie would be there. After Sun left Hong Kong, the two old friends never saw each other again until, by coincidence, the two met on the street in Honolulu. Sun was no longer practicing medicine but had become a revolutionary. He had cut his hair short and was wearing Western suits. Dr. Cantlie could hardly recognize him. But the two good friends were happy to see each other after all these years. Dr. Cantlie told Sun that he was going back to London and invited Sun to visit him if he should go to London.

This casual encounter was fateful. After Sun left Honolulu and arrived in San Francisco in June 1896 on his first visit to the U.S. mainland, the Manchu consul in the United States was closely watching his every movement with the intention of trapping him but was unable to do anything. On September 23, 1986, Sun left New York and sailed for London.

The Manchu consul in the United States immediately informed the Manchu legation in London. So shortly after Sun arrived there in October 1896, he was kidnapped and put under house arrest in the Manchu legation in London. The Manchu ambassador plotted to charter a boat to smuggle him back to China for execution, and Sun was in real danger. Luckily, he convinced a servant in the embassy to smuggle a note to Dr. Cantlie, who came to his rescue.

Dr. Cantlie wrote a letter to a London newspaper, the *Globe,* and news of the kidnapping quickly spread all over London. The public was indignant at the Manchu legation for committing such a violation of diplomatic privileges. The British Foreign Ministry and Scotland Yard intervened, and under pressure, the Manchu ambassador was forced to release Sun. This is the well-known story of "Kidnapped in London," written by Sun after his release.

SUN YAT-SEN'S SIX VISITS TO HAWAII, 1878–1910

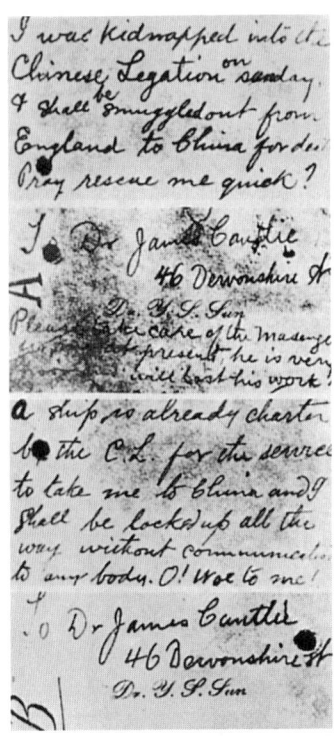

FIGURE 1.23. The notes Sun Yat-sen smuggled out to Dr. James Cantlie. Reproduced from *Mr. Sun Yat-sen* (Beijing: Museum of the History of the Chinese Revolution, 1986).

This incident made Sun a world-famous revolutionist. Sun said in his autobiography that it was truly lucky that Dr. Cantlie stopped over in Honolulu. Otherwise, "I would not have known that Cantlie had returned to London, and Cantlie would not have known that I would visit London."[33]

The address of the Manchu legation building was and today is still the same: 31 Portland Place, London W1N 3AG. After 1912, the Manchu legation became the embassy of the Republic of China. After 1950, it continued to be the embassy of the People's Republic of China. The room in which Sun was locked up has been kept as a special room in memory of Sun all these years. It is not open to the public but can be visited by special appointment with the Chinese embassy.

THE FIFTH VISIT (SEPTEMBER 1903–MARCH 1904): REORGANIZING THE HSING CHUNG HUI AND FOUNDING THE CHINESE REVOLUTIONARY ARMY

After Sun was released, he stayed in London for another few months. During this time, he studied the political system of Western democracy and finalized his

FIGURE 1.24. The room and the exterior view of the iron-bar window in the Manchu legation in London where Sun Yat-sen was locked up. Reproduced from *Mr. Sun Yat-sen* (Beijing: Museum of the History of the Chinese Revolution, 1986).

philosophy of "San Min Zhuyi" (Three Principles of the People) 三民主義, which became his political platform for the Chinese revolution. Then he traveled to Japan, Indochina, and Hong Kong.

In 1900, he organized the second uprising, the Waichou Uprising, which also failed. This was also the year the Boxer Rebellion broke out in China, and eight countries (six European countries, the United States, and Japan) joined together, invaded China, and occupied the Manchu capital, Peking. The Manchu emperor fled to Northwest China, and the whole country was in chaos. Again, the Manchu regime was defeated and kowtowed to the foreign powers. Another unequal treaty was signed, more territory was ceded, and more indemnities were paid to the foreign powers. This further aroused people all over China, and the revolutionary movement surged to a new high.

After traveling in Japan and French Indochina to rally overseas Chinese and raise funds, Sun returned once again to Hawaii in September 1903. His arrival was

FIGURE 1.25. News item in the *Pacific Commercial Advertiser,* October 7, 1903, reporting Sun Yat-sen's arrival in Honolulu. *See Apendix XI for complete news item.*

reported in the *Honolulu Pacific Commercial Advertiser* (today's *Honolulu Advertiser*) on October 7, 1903, under the headline: "Noted Reformer Sun Arrives Here Quietly," "Man Who Would Like to Overthrow the Dynasty of the Empress Dowager and Her Mandarins."

But, when Sun came back to Honolulu in 1903, he found that the Hsing Chung Hui he had established in 1894 had fallen under the influence of his political rival Liang Chi-chao, who together with Kang You-wei, was a monarchist. Kang and Liang started a reformist movement in China with the objective of setting up a constitutional monarchy. They failed and fled to Tokyo, where Liang met with Sun. Liang expressed his wish to cooperate with Sun and said he was going to Hawaii. Sun never suspected that Liang had ulterior motives, so he wrote a letter recommending Liang to his friends in Hawaii. In early 1900, Liang arrived in Hawaii and started to organize the Bao Wong Hui (Save the Monarch Society) 保皇會. He took advantage of the fact that he had a letter of recommendation from Sun and met with Sun Mei and other members of Hsing Chung Hui. Liang won over the majority, including Sun Mei, and established a Chinese newspaper called *Sun Chung Kwok Bo* (New China Daily News) to publicize his political views. Liang left Honolulu a few months later.[34] The Hsing Chung Hui in Hawaii was practically paralyzed.

Shortly after Sun returned to Honolulu in 1903, he started to fight back. He published an article in the *Tan San Sun Bo* (Hawaiian Chinese News), publicizing his political views and explaining the differences between his views and those of Liang Chi-chao. He won back most of his followers. By the end of 1903, on invitation of a Christian minister, Mao Man-ming, Sun visited Hilo. He went by boat to Ka'u on the island of Hawaii. There he met Lai Hip, a well-known Chinese merchant and a leader of the Chinese community in Hilo. Lai Hip and another Chinese merchant and owner of the Coffee Salon in Hilo, Wong Gum, headed the welcoming committee and accompanied Sun from Ka'u to Hilo by train. Later, they both became active followers of Sun. Sun stayed in their homes when he was in Hilo.[35] Sun was invited to make a public speech at the Japanese Theater in Hilo. Hundreds of people attended and listened to him. It was a big success. Sun said that this was the first time he had made a public speech to a big crowd of overseas Chinese. After that, he was invited to make more speeches. He went to the sugar plantations to talk to the workers, who responded with zest.

FIGURE 1.26. News item in the *Pacific Commercial Advertiser*, December 14, 1903, reporting Sun Yat-sen's speech to a Chinese audience the preceding day. *See Appendix XII for complete news item.*

FIGURE 1.27. The American Theatre in Honolulu's Chinatown where Sun Yat-sen spoke to a big crowd on December 14, 1903. Reproduced from *Historical Traces of Sun Yat-sen's Activities in Hong Kong, Macao and Overseas* (Hong Kong: United College, Chinese University of Hong Kong, and Ghuangzhou: Sun Yat-sen Research Institute, Zhongshan University, 1986).

Sun formed the first revolutionary organization in Hilo. Because the Hsing Chung Hui in Hawaii, under attack by the Bao Wong Hui, was no longer functioning, Sun changed the name of the Hilo organization to Chung Hua Keming Jun (Chinese Revolutionary Army) 中華革命軍. (The names of some of the members are listed in Appendix 6.) When the Hsing Chung Hui was first formed in 1894, its political platform included three slogans: drive away the Tartars, recover China for the Chinese, and establish a republic. Sun added a fourth slogan to the Chung Hua Keming Jun platform: equalize land ownership. This was an important development in Sun's thinking. He set his mind on reforming the centuries-old Chinese land-tenure system in which the peasants who tilled the land did not have land of their own. This four-slogan platform reflected the basic concepts Sun advocated in his San Min Zhuyi. Two years later, this platform became that of the Tung Meng Hui when it was formed in Tokyo.[36]

When Sun returned to Honolulu, his followers there also invited him to make public speeches. On December 13, 1903, Sun spoke to a big crowd at the American Theatre on Hotel Street in Chinatown. This event was reported by the *Pacific Commercial Advertiser* on December 14, 1903, under the headline: "Dr. Sun Advocates a Revolt in China." The news item reported details of Sun's speech and

FIGURE 1.28. In Honolulu's Chinatown today, the Maunakea Market Place is where the American Theatre used to stand. Picture taken in 1998. Photo by Yansheng Ma Lum.

commented: "Dr. Sun was received with great enthusiasm and his speech was frequently punctuated with applause. The theater was packed from pit to gallery and even the stage was crowded."

After that, Sun made many other public speeches, and every time he spoke, there was a big, enthusiastic crowd, and he won the support of many people in the Chinese community. The well-known businessman Lum Yip Kee recalled that when Sun Yat-sen made speeches in public asking the Chinese for support, he gave Sun moral support, and at the meetings when Sun made public speeches, he would arrange the table and drinks for Sun.[37]

In early 1904, the Hsing Chung Hui Honolulu chapter was reorganized into the Chung Hua Keming Jun (Chinese Revolutionary Army). The first meeting was held in the former See Dai Doo building, which was located on the old Vineyard Street in Honolulu. Sun's native village, Choy Hang, belonged to Dai Doo in Chungshang District. So Sun was considered a member of the See Dai Doo Society in Honolulu. When Sun visited Honolulu, he often went to the society. Sometimes, his friends would come to the society and seek medical treatment from Sun.[38]

Tan San Sun Bo and Chee Yow Shin Bo

The *Tan San Sun Bo* (Hawaiian Chinese News) was formed in 1883 and owned by Ching Wai-nam, one of Sun's relatives. It carried mostly business news. Sun made

FIGURE 1.29. When Sun visited Honolulu in 1904, the See Dai Doo Building was on Vineyard Street, near Liliha Street. This picture shows the old Society building after the second floor was renovated in 1915. Later, Vineyard Street was widened to become today's Vineyard Boulevard. The old building was demolished. Today, the See Dai Doo Society building is located on Pali Highway. Photograph courtesy of the See Dai Doo Society.

this paper the official newspaper of the Hsing Chung Hui, and Ho Fon was the editor. The newspaper office became a center where enthusiastic Chinese gathered and discussed issues regarding the revolution. The members of the Chinese-English Debating Society were the most active participants.[39]

A few years later, in 1907, Ching Wai-nam felt that he was unable to continue funding the newspaper, so Zane Chong-fook, a wealthy businessman and ardent supporter of Sun, bought it and changed its name to *Ming Sun Yat Bo*. It was then located at 1016 Smith Street, Honolulu. Sun recommended Loo Sun, a newspaperman from Hong Kong, to be the editor. On August 30, 1908, the name of the newspaper was changed to *Chee Yow Shin Bo* (Liberty News). It was located at 40 North Hotel Street, at the corner of Smith Street, in Chinatown. When Sun was in Honolulu, he spent a lot of time in the office of this newspaper. For many years to come, this newspaper continued to publicize Sun's views and played an important role in enhancing the cause of the revolution.[40]

FIGURE 1.30. The masthead of the Chinese newspaper *Tan San Sun Bo Loong Kee* (Hawaiian Chinese News). Reproduced from *The Chinese of Hawaii* (Honolulu, 1929).

FIGURE 1.31. The masthead of *Chee Yow Shin Bo* (Liberty News). Reproduction courtesy the Hawaii State Archives. The *Chee Yow Shin Bo* was located at 40 North Hotel Street, Honolulu. The postal notice printed in the paper, dated November 6, 1908, indicates the date of its establishment. Later, in 1910, when the Tung Meng Hui Hawaii chapter was formed, the first meeting was held in this newspaper office. Sun Yat-sen spent a lot of time in the office when he was in town. His son, Sun Fo, worked here as a translator. Reproduction courtesy of the Hawaii State Archives.

FIGURE 1.32. The old building on Hotel Street in which the office of *The Liberty News* was located. Photo reproduced from the *Historical Traces of Sun Yat-sen's Activities in Hong Kong, Macao and Overseas* (HK, 1986).

FIGURE 1.33. The 40 North Hotel Street site, near the corner of Smith Street, as it appeared in 1998. The old building was demolished. Photo by Yansheng Ma Lum.

FIGURE 1.34. Sun Yat-sen and his son, Sun Fo, taken in Honolulu in 1910. Reproduced from *Sun Yat-sen* (Shanghai: Shanghai Museum of Sun Yat-sen's Former Residence, 1996).

Joining the Ket On Society in Honolulu

During this visit, on November 24, 1903, Sun joined the Ket On Society of Hawaii. The Ket On Society belonged to the Hoong Moon Fraternity 洪門會, whose history in China could be traced back to the seventeenth century. The Hoong Moon members vowed to "overthrow the Manchu and restore the Ming." So Sun and the Hoong Moon Fraternity shared the same objectives. Most overseas Chinese in the United States were members of the Hoong Moon Fraternity, and the name of their organization was the Chee Kung Tong 致公堂, also known as the Chinese Free Masons. By joining the Ket On Society in Hawaii, Sun became a fraternity brother of all the Chee Kung Tong members in the United States, and he won them over to support the revolution. In April 1904, Sun made his second fund-raising tour in the United States. Wong San-duck, the president of the Chee Kung Tong, accompanied him during his tour all over the United States, introducing him to Chee Kung Tong members, who gathered to hear Sun talk about the revolution and generously contributed to support it.[41]

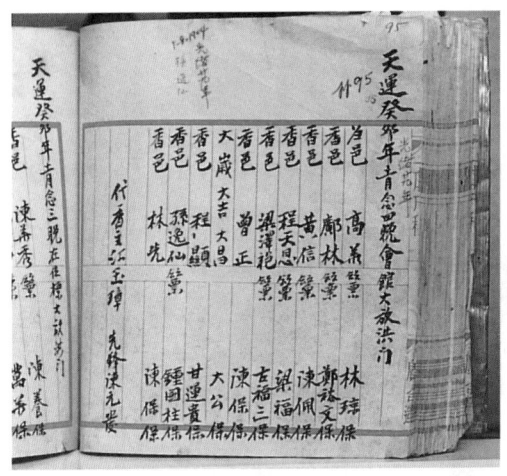

FIGURE 1.35. The Ket On Society record in which Sun's name is listed among the persons who joined the organization. His sponsor was Chung Kwok-chee, another name of Chung Mookheen. Photo courtesy of the Ket On Society, Honolulu.

THE SIXTH VISIT (MARCH 1910–MAY 1910): FORMING THE TUNG MENG HUI HAWAII CHAPTER

After his visit to the United States, Sun headed for Japan. In August 1905, he reorganized the Hsing Chung Hui in Tokyo to form the Tung Meng Hui (Alliance Society). Its political platform was the same four-slogan platform Sun developed in 1903 when he formed the Chung Hua Keming Jun in Hilo. This was another important milestone in the revolutionary movement as the Tung Meng Hui developed into the most important political party in China. Within a year of its formation, there were ten thousand enrolled members, and in every province of China, there was a branch of the party. Branches were also organized in Europe, Southeast Asia, the United States, Canada, and Hawaii. With the establishment of the Tung Meng Hui, the revolution spread like wildfire. From Hsing Chung Hui to Tung Meng Hui, a powerful political party that would lead the Chinese revolution to victory was born.

From 1907 to 1908, Sun traveled in Singapore and French Indochina. He tapped the financial resources of the overseas Chinese in Southeast Asia and launched six armed uprisings. But all failed, and Sun said in his autobiography: "After the uprisings failed one after the other, I lost all the bases neighboring China, and I could not stay in this area any longer. I decided to roam all over again to raise funds for further action."[42]

In February 1910, Sun came back to the United States and organized Tung Meng Hui chapters in New York, Chicago, and San Francisco. Shortly after that, he returned to Hawaii in March and established the Tung Meng Hui Hawaii chapter. When he arrived in Honolulu, he was welcomed by a big crowd led by Loo Sun, the editor of the *Chee Yow Shin Bo,* Zane Chong-fook, and Loui Kwan-jun. Sun was invited to speak at the Chinese Theater in Honolulu. Almost two thousand people gathered to listen to him. Sun talked about the Canton New Army Up-

FIGURE 1.36. The site of 177 North King Street, where Ching Chow's store used to be, as it appeared in 1998. The building was built in 1905 and so is the same building in which Sun once stayed in 1910. The store space was rented by different owners over the years. Photo by Yansheng Ma Lum.

rising, which was launched in February 1910. He said that although this uprising failed again, another one would soon be staged, and he was optimistic that this one would succeed. People were greatly encouraged by his speech and their spirits soared. Later, a meeting was held at the office of the *Chee Yow Shin Bo*. More than twenty people attended this first meeting, and the Tung Meng Hui Hawaii chapter was formed.[43] The names of the participants are listed in Appendix 7.

When he was in Hawaii, Sun appeared in public and made speeches to hundreds of people, but the Manchu consul never stopped watching his every move. He had to keep his daily agenda secret, and he never stayed in any one place for too long. Many members of the Tung Meng Hui in Hawaii sheltered him. For example, he once stayed in the home of Loui Kwan-jun, a wealthy businessman and a member of the Tung Meng Hui, in 1910. Owen Loui, Loui Kwan-jun's son, remembered hearing his father talking about Sun's "hiding in their home."[44] Another time, Sun stayed in the room on the second floor of Ching Chow's store, the Wing Hong Yuen Company, located at 177 North King Street. He also stayed many times in Ching Chow's home, located at 1127C Banyan Street, near Palama. The house now is a private residence.[45]

How people kept the whereabouts of Sun a secret when he was in town was well described by Alfred Pierce Taylor. In his article, "Sun Yat Sen in Honolulu," he said that he was fortunate to be the one newspaperman in Honolulu to inter-

FIGURE 1.37. The Lum Yip Kee Building at 80 North King Street in Honolulu, photographed in 1998. Photo by Yansheng Ma Lum.

view Sun in the summer of 1910. (In the article, the year is given as 1911. Since Sun's last visit to Honolulu was March–May 1910 and he was in San Francisco in 1911, the interview probably occurred in the summer of 1910.) Taylor wrote:

> Mysterious tips had reached me by telephone . . . that he was in town again. I knew where to begin my quest, for he had many blood cousins living in the island capital. At his cousin's house, in a dark, remote lane, I was told, almost curtly, that he was not in Honolulu at all. I called at the newspaper office, and was told he was in a distant land. At a Chinese grocery store, I was similarly informed. But when I started again for the newspaper office, just around the corner, a mysterious, unknown man whispered, advising me to try the Liberty News again.
>
> Once more I passed through the outer door, dodging the line of type cases and then mounted a dark, narrow, creaky stairway, gaining the almost dark second floor, I went straight to the door of the little editorial office. Before I encountered anyone, I opened it. . . . and there was Sun Yat-sen sitting at the desk. . . .[46]

Sun was not the only one who had to take precautions. Special arrangements were also made to protect those well-known merchants and businessmen who joined the Tung Meng Hui. A secret chapter of Tung Meng Hui was formed in 1910. The first meeting was held at the home of C. K. Ai, and Young Kwong-tat was elected chairman of this secret chapter. Young Kwong-tat's son, Young Wah-duck, said that his father owned the store Kwang Cheong Lung at the corner of King Street and Maunakea Street in Honolulu's Chinatown. Tung Meng Hui members held their activ-

FIGURE 1.38. Elizabeth Lai Hip Lum, 96 years old. Photo taken in 1998 by Yansheng Ma Lum.

ities in this store. In 1951, Frank Eng, the owner of Eng Brothers Men's Clothing, rented the store space and found a dug-out basement. A neighbor told Eng that when Sun Yat-sen was in town, he and his followers held their activities here. This store space today is part of the Lum Yip Kee Building, located at 80 North King Street.[47]

Sun visited Hilo again in 1910 and spent almost two weeks there. The Chinese Revolutionary Army in Hilo was reorganized, and all members became Tung Meng Hui members; 385 members joined and were organized into two companies, four platoons, and twenty-four squads as in the army.[48] The names of the leaders are listed in Appendix 8.

When Sun was in Hilo, he often visited Lai Hip at his residence. The only surviving daughter of Lai Hip, Elizabeth Lai Hip Lum, met Sun at her home. Mrs. Lai Hip Lum is now ninety-six years old and her mind is still sharp. Today, she is practically the only person who had met Sun Yat-sen in person and is still coherent enough to tell the story. Although she was only eight years old at the time she met Sun, she had such a pleasant impression of him that to the present day she can still remember that visit quite vividly. Elizabeth said that she recalled Sun being "a handsome man and a wonderful person." She said Dr. Sun was very friendly, laughing and talking with her, asking her all kinds of questions, such as how she liked school. Her mother told her not to bother Dr. Sun, but Sun said, "let her stay." It was a long visit. She was so happy and she danced round and round.[49]

On Maui, a Tung Meng Hui Maui chapter was also formed, and Dang Mingsan, Lau Pang, and others joined.[50]

Wen Phong-fei, an overseas Chinese in San Francisco, was hired to come to Honolulu to be the editor of *Chee Yow Shin Bo* in 1910–1911. He went back to China in 1911, and he published three articles in Beijing when he was eighty years old. In these articles, which were first tape-recorded and then transcribed for publication, he said that when Sun was in Honolulu, he visited the newspaper office quite often and gave directions as to how to improve the editing of the newspaper. Sun told them not to talk about the revolution in terms of theory but in terms of the oppression people suffered under Manchu rule. This, the common people could easily relate to. When Sun made speeches to the public, Wen used to accompany him. Wen said that Sun always spoke in simple language that the people could understand, and he could sway the emotions of the audience. After a speech, many people would ask to join the Tung Meng Hui and many gave donations.[51]

In a short period, Tung Meng Hui membership in Hawaii expanded to almost one thousand. As compared to 1894, when Sun first organized the Hsing Chung Hui, people's revolutionary spirit soared and more and more people joined the organization.

Wen Phong-fei also said in his memoir that Sun drafted an application form for the Tung Meng Hui so that after a speech, people could sign the form and become members. Wen said that he saw stacks and stacks of signed application forms in the office of the *Chee Yow Shin Bo*.[52] One could see how enthusiastic people were in joining the Tung Meng Hui.

In his letter of April 8, 1910, addressed to Tung Meng Hui members in New York, Sun said:

> It was one week now since I arrived in Honolulu. There were 2,000 people gathered to welcome me. People were in high spirits as compared to a few years ago. One evening, after the gathering, there were more than one hundred people crowding in the office of the *Chee Yow Shin Bo*, asking to join the Tung Meng Hui. . . .
>
> The comrades in Honolulu simplify the procedure by printing out application forms so that those who want to join just put down their name, where they come from, the date and their signature. Over a hundred members can sign the application form and join in one evening. This procedure invented by the Honolulu comrades is a good one that can be emulated by other cities. For the revolutionary tides are surging forth, more and more people will be aroused to join our ranks.[53]

In 1912, official membership cards were issued to the Tung Meng Hui Hawaii chapter members. (See Figures 1.39 and 1.40)

Before Sun left Honolulu, he advised his Hawaiian followers to set up a Chinese language school. After he left, Young Kwong-tat, C. K. Ai, Zane Chong-fook, and other sponsors donated money to set up the Wah Mun School.[54] This school was renamed Chung Shan School in 1928 to commemorate Sun.

Today, Young Kwong-tat's son, Young Wah-duck, is the president of the school.

SUN RETURNS TO CHINA

In May 1910, Sun left Honolulu. Francis W. Damon was the master of ceremonies at a gathering to see him off.[55] This was the last time that Sun sojourned in Hawaii. One and a half years later, the October 10th Wuchang Uprising succeeded. Sun returned to China and was sworn in as the first president of the Republic of China on January 1, 1912.

After the establishment of the Republic of China, the United States became

FIGURE 1.39. The Tung Meng Hui membership card of Hee Tong, who was one of the first to join. The card reads: Hee Tong had sworn allegiance To the Hui and paid membership Fee. The card was the twentieth issued by the secretary of the Tung Meng Hui Hawaii chapter, Young Kwong-tat (signed). Date: May 11, 1912. Photo courtesy of Young Wah-duck.

FIGURE 1.40. Lum Chee's Tung Meng Hui membership card was the 848th issued by Young Kwong-tat (signed) and Lai Hip (signed), the secretary of the Tung Meng Hui Hilo chapter, May 29, 1912. As a rule, members in Honolulu got their membership cards first, followed by members on the outer islands. Hilo members might be the last to get their cards. As there were 385 members in Hilo, the membership card issued to Lum Chee was number 848, which was close to the thousand mark. This fits with the fact that there were around one thousand members in Hawaii at the time. Reproduced from Lum Chee's collection.

FIGURE 1.41. Chung Shan School, Honolulu, as it appeared in 1998. Photo by Yansheng Ma Lum.

the first country to recognize the new government. At that time, Prince Kuhio was the Territory of Hawaii delegate to the U.S. Congress. Chinese community members in Hawaii cabled him and asked his assistance in procuring recognition of the new Republic of China. Prince Kuhio took active steps to encourage the United States government to extend the desired recognition.[56]

After the government of the Republic of China was inaugurated in Nanking in January 1912, Sun faced the difficult task of establishing a unified and democratic government in China. The Manchu government still controlled North China, and the emperor was still in power in Peking. In order to unify the country, Sun Yat-sen held negotiations with Yuan Shih-kai, who was then the commander of the Imperial Army in Peking. Yuan agreed to cooperate with Sun to force the emperor to abdicate on condition that Yuan should be the president of the new government. For the peaceful unification of China, Sun agreed to resign his presidency in favor of Yuan. On April 1, 1912, Sun officially left office. The Manchu emperor abdicated, and Yuan became the president. Soon after, he abused the constitution and began his dictatorial rule.

For the next decade, China was in turmoil again. In 1913, Sun Yat-sen started the Second Revolution against Yuan but was defeated and had to leave the country and go to Japan. In Japan, he reorganized the Kuomintang into the Chinese Revolutionary Party. By the end of 1915, Yuan Shih-kai had restored the monarchy with himself as "emperor." The whole country was against him, and he died a few months later. By this time, warlords in different regions of China had seized local power and were fighting against each other, turning the whole country into a war zone.

FIGURE 1.42. Sun Yat-sen at the time he was sworn in as provisional president of the Republic of China in January 1912. Photo reproduced from *Sun Yat-sen* (Shanghai: Shanghai Museum of Sun Yat-sen's Former Residence, 1996).

Sun returned to China after Yuan died. On August 27, 1917, he assumed the title of generalissimo of the Military Government of the Republic of China in Kwangtung Province and launched the Third Revolution to reinstate the constitution. On May 5, 1921, Sun Yat-sen assumed the post of emergency president in Canton. In 1922, the warlord in Kwangtung Province, Chen Jiong-ming, staged a coup against Sun, trying to capture and kill him. Sun managed to escape to Shanghai. In the years that followed, he exerted himself to the utmost in the efforts to start a military expedition against the warlords and establish a democratic government. He fell ill, however, and during a trip to the north to negotiate with the warlords for peaceful unification of the country, he died of liver cancer in Peking on March 12, 1925. His dying words were: "Peace, Struggle and Save China."

Sun died not only as a great pioneer, a great revolutionist, and a great patriot but also as a man of high moral virtue. Throughout his career, he never seized personal power; he never grabbed personal wealth; and he never indulged in nepotism or favoritism.

Sun's resignation in favor of Yuan Shih-kai was an example of his attitude toward personal power. Some would say that Sun should not have compromised with Yuan, but his action fully demonstrated that he was not a politician hungry for personal power. For the good of the country, he was willing to give up his position as president.

Sun died with no personal wealth. He once said: "I never cared for money. Money was one thing that caused China's disasters."[57] When his will was drawn up shortly before he died, Sun said that he never accumulated any personal wealth. All he had was a few personal effects, which he left to his wife, Madame Soong

Ching Ling. His residence in Shanghai, now the Shanghai Museum of Sun Yat-sen's Former Residence, was donated by overseas Chinese.

One striking example he set in opposing nepotism and favoritism was his refusal to appoint Sun Mei as the governor of Kwangtung Province. Sun Mei gave almost all his wealth to support the revolution. Shortly after Sun became president in 1912, a group of followers, including many overseas Chinese, signed a petition asking Sun to nominate Sun Mei as governor of Kwangtung Province. Sun did not approve the nomination. He made excuses, saying that his brother was a good businessman but not a politician, so he did not think he was fit for that position.

Sun Yat-sen was a great man indeed.

THE MYSTERY OF SUN YAT-SEN'S BIRTH CERTIFICATE

Sun was a revolutionary fugitive with a price on his head, and the Manchu regime never stopped pursuing him. He disguised himself under all kinds of pseudonyms. On one occasion when he went to Japan, he identified himself as "Mr. Aloha from Hawaii."[58]

In 1897, when he was in Tokyo, he picked up a Japanese name, Nakayama, from a nameplate on a house he passed. In Chinese, Nakayama is read as Chung Shan 中山. This is how his name Sun Chung-shan came about.[59] In China, people call him by this name, although his official name is Sun Wen 孫文. When he signed letters and documents in Chinese, he used the name Sun Wen. When he signed letters and documents in English, he used the name Sun Yat-sen.

After the failure of the First Canton Uprising, Sun narrowly escaped to Japan in 1896. He cut his hair short and dressed like a Japanese and passed as one. In the article "My Reminiscences," published in 1912, Sun said:

> I have seen it stated that I had Malay blood, and also that I was born in Honolulu. Both these statements are false. I am purely Chinese, but after the Japanese war, when the Japanese began to be treated with more respect, I had no trouble in passing for a Japanese. I admit I owe a great deal to this circumstance, as otherwise I would not have escaped many dangerous situations.[60]

To facilitate Sun's traveling to the United States, especially after the U.S. Congress passed the Chinese Exclusion Act of 1882, which barred Chinese from entering the country, his brother Sun Mei and his friends managed to secure for him a birth certificate issued by the Territory of Hawaii stating that he was born "at Waimalu, Ewa, Oahu, on the 24th day of November, 1870."

Neil L. Thomsen, who worked at the National Archives–Pacific Sierra Region, wrote an article, "No Such Sun Yat-sen,"[61] telling how he looked into the box containing the files of people arriving at the Port of San Francisco on board the SS *Korea* on April 6, 1904. He found a file jacket without any documentary contents in it, but on it was the faded pencil mark: "No Such Sun Yat-sen." He could not help but be curious and was determined to solve the mystery. He searched

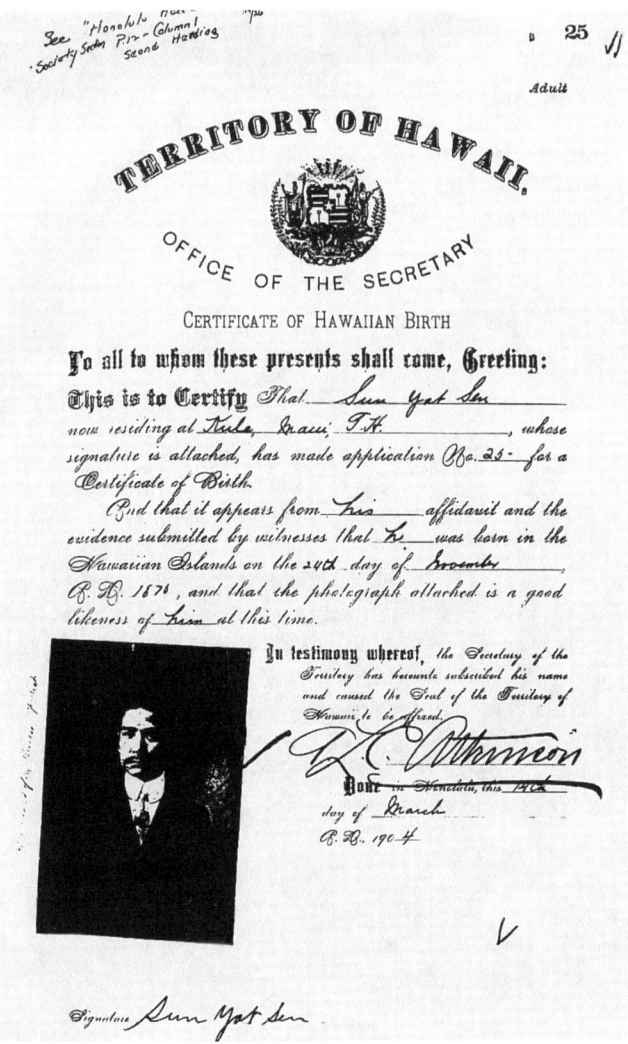

FIGURE 1.43. Birth certificate of Sun Yat-sen issued by the Territory of Hawaii. Photo courtesy of the National Archives–Pacific Sierra Region, San Bruno, California.

for five years and finally located the file in the National Archives–Southeast Region in Atlanta.

The file was rightfully returned to the National Archives–Pacific Sierra Region in San Bruno, California. Thomsen looked into the case file and found Sun's birth certificate issued by the secretary of the Territory of Hawaii on March 4, 1904.

Also included was "a Hawaiian Territorial passport" documenting Sun's status as an American citizen.

There was something in the file that was most interesting: That was a letter of April 15, 1904, from the Office of the Commissioner, Immigration Service, to the Chinese inspector in charge, San Francisco. In this letter was a summary of Sun's statement to the effect that "he waived his right to American citizenship and was ... a subject of China."

Therefore, it is beyond a reasonable doubt that Sun did have a birth certificate issued by the Territory of Hawaii, and he tried to correct the fraud by "waiving his American citizenship."

Of course, this had serious ramifications, for he was "refused admission to the United States" and was held incommunicado in the wooden immigration shed in San Francisco for more than ten days before his friends from the Chee Kung Tong in San Francisco could help him file an appeal. He was finally permitted to land and proceeded with his second fund-raising tour in the United States, a happy ending of the mystery of Sun Yat-sen's birth certificate.

TWO

Sun Yat-sen's
Fund-Raising in Hawaii

HAWAII'S CONTRIBUTIONS TO THE TEN UPRISINGS

Sun Yat-sen organized ten armed uprisings against the Manchu regime before the October 10, 1911 Wuchang Uprising, which finally overthrew the Manchu regime. These were:

1. The Canton Uprising, October 26, 1895; more than three hundred people participated, more than sixty were arrested, and five sacrificed their lives.
2. The Waichou Uprising, October 8–22, 1900; more than six hundred participated, and later more than twenty thousand people joined in.
3. The Chiuchou Uprising, May 22–27, 1907; more than seven hundred people participated; seventy-seven died in combat, and more than seventy were arrested and executed.
4. The Waichou Chi-nu-hu Uprising, June 2–13, 1907; more than one hundred participated.
5. The Fangcheng Uprising, September 1–17, 1907; more than three hundred participated, and later more than one thousand people joined in.
6. The Zhen-nan-guan Uprising, December 1–8, 1907; eighty people participated, and more than one hundred soldiers from the Manchu army surrendered.
7. The Chinlian Uprising, March 27–May 3, 1908; more than two hundred people participated; four died in combat, and two were wounded.
8. The Hekou Uprising, April 29–May 26, 1908; more than three hundred people participated, and more than three thousand soldiers from the Manchu army surrendered.
9. The Canton New Army Uprising, February 12, 1910; more than one hundred people died in combat, and fourteen were arrested.
10. The Canton Wong Fa Gong Uprising, April 27 (March 29 according to the Chinese lunar calendar), 1911; one thousand seven hundred and ninety people participated, and eighty-six died in combat or were executed.[1]

To organize these uprisings, Sun went all over the world to raise funds from the overseas Chinese with which to purchase weapons and ammunition and to pay salaries to the officers and men. The first place he went was Hawaii; his first attempt to raise money started in Honolulu, and the first uprising he organized was mainly funded by the Chinese in Hawaii.

After the First Canton Uprising of 1895 failed, Sun fled China. During more than sixteen years in exile, he traveled all over the world, spreading his ideas about the revolution and raising funds to support new uprisings against the Manchus. Whenever he had difficulties and was in urgent need of funds, he always turned to the Chinese in Hawaii for help, and they never failed him. After the Republic of China was inaugurated January 1, 1912, the revolution did not end. Sun continued to strive for a united and democratic China, and he continued to solicit support from the overseas Chinese.

There are no accurate records of how much money the Chinese in Hawaii contributed to the revolutionary movement led by Sun Yat-sen. One source, however, says that from 1894 to 1925, the Chinese in Hawaii contributed a total of US$250,000 in support of the revolution led by Sun Yat-sen. This figure was provided by Chock Lun, who was the editor of *The Chinese of Hawaii,* 1929 edition. In the 1936 edition of *The Chinese of Hawaii,* he published an article, "Chinese Organizations in Hawaii," in which he wrote:

> From the time of the organization of the Hsing Chung Hui 45 years ago until 1925, when Dr. Sun died, members of the local Kuomintang (Note by author: this should be read as including all organizations, namely the Hsing Chung Hui, the Chunghua Keming Jun, the Teng Meng Hui and in 1912, the Kuomintang.) had contributed at least US$250,000 gold in support of Dr. Sun's revolutionary movements and wars against his political opponents in China.[2]

FUNDING THE FIRST CANTON UPRISING

The funds for the First Canton Uprising came mainly from the Hsing Chung Hui members in Hawaii. Aside from the five dollars each member paid as a membership fee, Sun issued Hsing Chung Hui bonds at one hundred dollars each, to be repaid tenfold after the revolution succeeded. The issuance of the bonds was registered in the 1893 Issue of the "Register of Special Bonds" in Honolulu.

Sun collected $1,100 from the sale of bonds and $288 from membership fees. That was not enough to fund an uprising. Dang Yum-nam, a merchant in Honolulu and Sun's close friend, liquidated his personal assets and donated a large sum of money to buy weapons. Sun Mei, Sun Yat-sen's brother, sold his cattle and donated the money. Sun used the 13,000 Hong Kong dollars (US$6,000) from Hawaii and plus other funds he raised in Hong Kong and used it to launch the First Canton Uprising.[3]

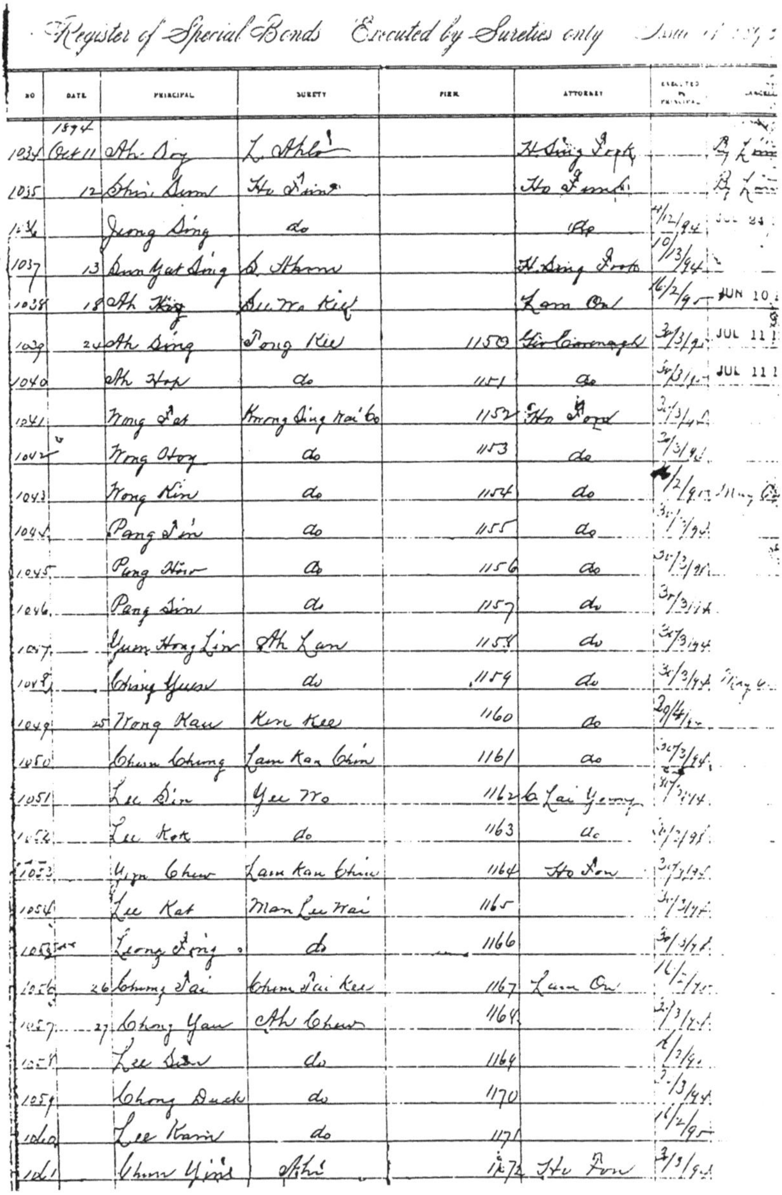

FIGURE 2.1. A page of the 1893 issue of the "Register of Special Bonds." No. 1037 lists Sun Yat-sen in the column "Principal," and his borther Sun Mei's name appears in the column "Surety." Reproduction courtesy of the State Archives of Hawaii.

FIGURE 2.2. The Hsing Chung Hui bond Sun Yat-sen issued in 1894. On the certificate are the signatures of Sun Yat-sen, the president, and Lau Cheong, who was elected president of the Hsing Chung Hui at its first meeting. Lau signed "for the treasurer." This bond was kept by Mrs. En Fon Lee, daughter-in-law of Lee To-ma. The Hsing Chung Hui Ledger recorded that Lee bought bonds worth one hundred dollars. Reproduced from *Five Hsing Chung Hui Men of Valor*, courtesy of the Hawaii Chinese History Center.

THE SECOND UPRISING

The second uprising, the Waichou Uprising, staged in 1900, was funded mainly by donations from Chinese in Hong Kong and a Japanese supporter. Sun Mei was the only one in Hawaii involved in the funding of this uprising. In a letter addressed to his friend Wu Jing-heng (Wu Zhi-hui), dated October 30, 1909, Sun said:

> In 1900, when the Waichow Uprising was launched, we needed at least one hundred thousand dollars or more. I got some from Hong Kong, some from Japan.... I relied on my brother for help. My brother and I had donated all we had.... Two years ago, my brother filed for bankruptcy.... I am the one responsible for his bankruptcy....[4]

There is no record of the total amount of money that Sun Mei donated. However, according to one source, Hou Chung-yi, Sun Fo's secretary, claimed that he heard in a Sun family discussion that Sun Mei's total contributions amounted to approximately $700,000.[5]

THE THIRD THROUGH EIGHTH UPRISINGS, 1907–1908

The funding of the third through the eighth uprisings came from the overseas Chinese in Southeast Asia, Japan, Europe, Canada, the United States, and Hawaii. Lai Hip of Hilo sent $1,150.[6]

Lum Chee, father of co-author Raymond Lum, was a general merchandise store owner in Hilo and a loyal supporter of Sun Yat-sen. He joined in the activities of the Chung Hua Kemin Jun in Hilo in 1903 and later the Tung Meng Hui in 1910. He bought military bonds and donated money on many occasions. Fortunately, he understood the historical significance of these bonds, receipts, and other memorabilia of the revolution and kept them in the safe of his store. Before he died in 1941, he told Raymond to keep all these precious documents carefully and one day donate them to China. In 1985 Raymond Lum went to Beijing and donated the originals of the whole collection to the Sun Chung-shan Society in Beijing. The Chinese newspaper *People's Daily of China* (overseas edition) reported the news in its August 26, 1985 issue (Appendix 9). Now the originals of the bonds and receipts and other memorabilia of the revolution are kept in the Museum of the Revolutionary History of the Chinese People, which is located in Tian An Men Square in Beijing. The letter of September 14, 1911, written and signed by Sun, was reproduced in the *Collection of Sun Yat-sen's Manuscript—Letters,* published by the Wen Wu Chu Ban She in Beijing in 1986.

By studying Lum Chee's collection, one can get a glimpse of how Sun Yat-sen raised money in Hawaii and how the Chinese community contributed to the revolution.

In Lum Chee's collection, there is a receipt for a donation of $20 dated November 4, 1907, a donation to support one of the uprisings staged during 1907–1908. During these two years, Sun Yat-sen was in French Indochina and issued military bonds worth one hundred thousand dollars to raise funds for six uprisings.

What is special about this receipt is that it carries a serial number identifying it as a bond issued in "Tongkin, Annam." The Chinese characters on the receipt are incomplete but are clear enough to show that the bond Lum Chee bought was one of those Sun issued in French Indochina. Of course, Lum Chee was not the only one in Hilo that bought the bonds. The $20 he paid constituted a fraction of the $1,150 Lai Hip sent to Hong Kong headquarters. This receipt shows how well organized Sun's fund-raising efforts were. Even when Sun was in French Indochina, he still kept in touch with the Chinese in Hawaii and asked them to buy bonds he issued all over the world.

THE NINTH UPRISING

The ninth uprising was mainly funded by the overseas Chinese in the United States and Canada. There is no record of how much money Hawaii contributed to this uprising.

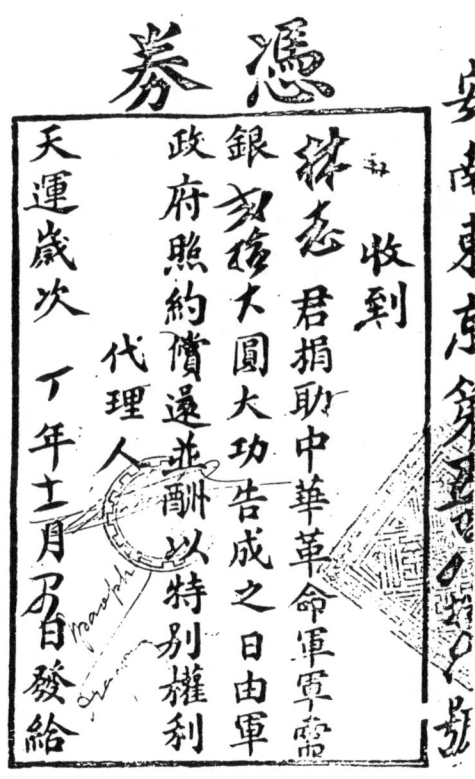

FIGURE 2.3. Lum Chee's November 4, 1907 receipt for a donation to the Chinese revolution. The receipt reads: "This is to acknowledge receipt of US$20.00 from Mr. Lum Chee, donated to the Chinese Revolutionary Army for military use, to be repaid by the Military Government with other special privileges. Date: Nov. 4, 1907." Reproduced from the Lum Chee collection.

THE TENTH UPRISING

The funding of the tenth uprising, the famous Wong Fa Gong Uprising of March 29, 1911, came exclusively from overseas Chinese all over the world. It was recorded that the Chinese of Hawaii donated US$2,000 to this uprising.[7] Another source says that Hawaii donated US$3,000.[8]

FIRST MILITARY BOND ISSUED IN HAWAII

In order to raise funds, Sun issued a number of military bonds, which were debenture certificates that promised the buyer repayment ten times or more, plus special privileges after the revolution succeeded. Obviously, the purpose was to provide incentives so that people would buy more bonds. However, experience showed that people were more concerned about incrimination than about the incentives. Many people were afraid to buy bonds because they did not want the Manchu consuls to find out and send word back home to persecute their relatives in China. Some bought the bonds but destroyed them to avoid incrimination, never intending to claim repayment.

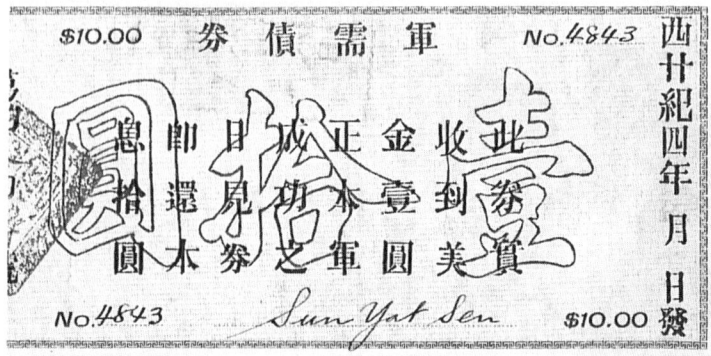

FIGURE 2.4. The military bond issued in 1904. The text reads: "US$1.00 paid, to be paid back US$10.00 the day the Army succeeds. Date: 1904. [signed] Sun Yat-sen." Reproduced from the Lum Chee colection.

Sun issued the first military bonds in Hawaii in 1904. These bonds were al printed in Honolulu. Sales of these bonds were not as good as expected, however and only $2,000 was collected. Not a big sum, but around the turn of the century, this was still a considerable amount of money. When Sun left Honolulu, he took the unsold bonds to San Francisco and collected another $4,000.[9]

DONATIONS FROM THE BROAD MASSES OF THE PEOPLE

Those who supported Sun Yat-sen came from all walks of life in the Chinese community. Some were wealthy merchants who donated large sums of money. The majority of Sun's supporters, however, were from the lower middle class, workers, intellectuals, and small merchants. They were not wealthy, but considering their means, they were most generous in supporting the revolution. To win the support of the broad masses of the people, Sun talked about the oppressive Manchu regime and advocated the establishment of a modern China. This appealed to the majority of the overseas Chinese, rich or poor, who suffered racial discrimination in the countries in which they resided. They wholeheartedly supported Sun's efforts to build a strong and prosperous China that they could be proud of and a democratic government that would protect their legal rights.

There are many moving stories of how the broad masses of the people responded to Sun's appeals and donated the little money they had. Wen Phong-fei, the editor of the *Chee Yow Hsin Bo* in Honolulu from 1910 to 1911, said in his memoir that many people came to the newspaper office to donate money. One day, a worker came and donated twenty dollars, although his monthly salary was only a little more than that. He was so sincere that "tears welled up in my eyes," Wen said.[10]

In Honolulu, there were eighteen Chinese students who donated two hundred dollars every month. Each of them would give a little more than ten dollars every month while their monthly allowances were only some twenty to thirty dollars.[11]

Young Wah-duck, whose father was Young Kwong-tat, the president of the Tung Meng Hui Hawaii chapter, said in an interview that his father, after receiving a letter or telegram from Sun asking for donations, would go to the bank to borrow a sum of money to send to Sun. Afterward, he would go to the members to collect the money to pay back the loan. He said that in those days, no one had that much money. It was with the support of many people, with a little donation from each, that he was able to repay the loan.[12]

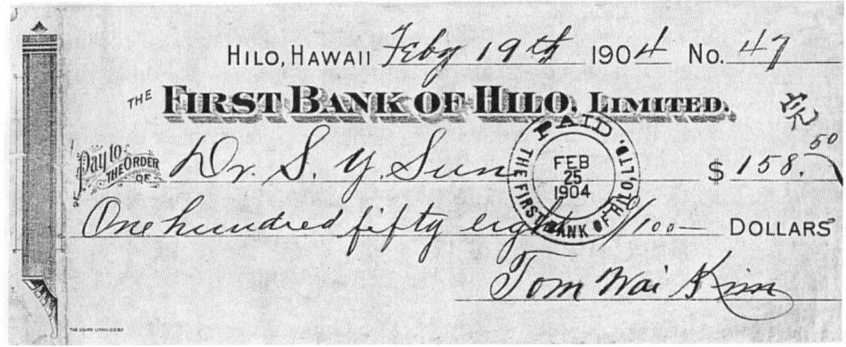

FIGURE 2.5. February 19, 1904, check to Sun Yat-sen, signed by Tom Wai-gum, representing donations by more than ten members of the Chung Hua Kemin Jun in Hilo. Reproduced from the Lum Chee collection.

FIGURE 2.6. The reverse side of the check to Sun Yat-sen, February 19, 1904, bears the signatures of Sun Yat-sen and Ho Fon, the chairman of the Hsing Chung Hui, who cashed it on February 25. Reproduced from the Lum Chee collection.

One item in Lum Chee's collection is a canceled check dated February 19, 1904, made to the order of S. Y. Sun in the amount $158.50. The check was signed by Tom Wai-gum, who was one of the members of the Chung Hua Kemin Jun in Hilo. He collected the sum from more than ten members and wrote the check to Sun. On the reverse side of the check are the signatures of Sun and Ho Fon, the chairman of the Hsing Chung Hui. This check, cashed on February 25, 1904, is one example of small donations from the masses.

There is a moving story about how the Chinese in Victoria and Toronto, Canada, raised money to support the revolution. In February 1911, when Sun was on his third visit to the United States, he went to Victoria to raise money. The members of the Chee Kung Tong in Victoria were mostly workers and did not have much money. As each worker could make only a small donation at a time, it would take a while before they could collect a large sum. As an uprising was scheduled to be launched and the need of money was urgent, the members agreed to mortgage their property, the tong building, for thirty thousand Hong Kong dollars and donated the sum to support the forthcoming uprising, scheduled for March that year. In the meantime, they collected money from members to pay back the mortgage. When the Chee Kung Tong members in Toronto heard about this, they also mortgaged their society building and donated ten thousand Hong Kong dollars.[13]

FOUR LETTERS TO HAWAII ASKING FOR DONATIONS

In 1910, Sun wrote four letters to Honolulu and Hilo, asking members of the Tung Meng Hui to help raise money for the revolution. These letters were dated June 1910; July 19, 1910; August 29, 1910; and October 16, 1910.

In 1910, Sun left Honolulu and arrived in Japan on board SS *Mongolia* on June 10. By mid-June, he wrote the first of the four letters. It was addressed to comrades of the Tung Meng Hui in Hawaii. In this letter, he asked for at least US$1,000 a month for the purpose of setting up a secret office in Tokyo. He said in the letter: "There are more than one thousand Tung Meng Hui members in Hawaii. If every member would donate one dollar a month, at least one thousand dollars could be collected every month." He also said that this money was to meet the urgent need of setting up a secret office in Tokyo for a period of maybe only one year, for he expected the revolution to succeed within this year. Then there would be no need to continue the donations.[14]

On July 19, 1910, Sun wrote the second letter addressed to "comrades of Honolulu and Hilo." In this letter he said he had arrived in Singapore from Japan and reiterated the need for providing money every month and said that the funds raised would be used "in the South" instead of for setting up the secret office in Tokyo.[15]

On August 29, 1910, Sun wrote the third letter, a long letter of four pages, addressed to "president of the Tung Meng Hui Kwok-ming and other comrades." Kwok-ming was another name of Lai Hip, who was the leader of the Tung Meng Hui, in Hilo. In this letter, Sun said that he had arrived in Penang in the Malay

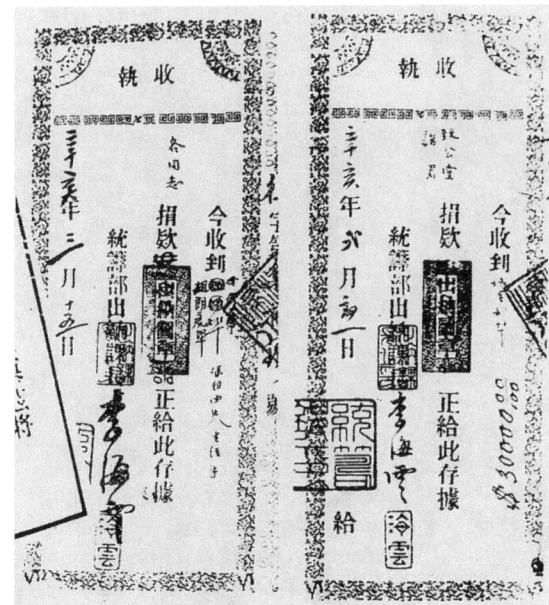

FIGURE 2.7. Receipts issued in 1911 for donations received from Victoria and Toronto, Canada. The Victoria receipt reads: "This is to acknowledge receipt of $30,000 from the gentlemen of Chee Kung Tong, Victoria. From the Fund-Raising Headquarters, [signed] Lee Hai Yun. Date: Feb. 1, 1911." The Toronto receipt, dated March 15, 1911, is basically the same except that the amount received was $10,000 and name of the donor was Chee Kung Tong, Toronto. Reproduced from *Mr. Sun Zhong-shan* (Beijing: Museum of Revolutionary History, 1986).

Peninsula. He explained why and how urgently he needed financial support and asked the comrades in Hawaii to do their best to help. The letter reads in part:

> I have asked you to raise funds for setting up a secret office in the North and now the need in the South becomes more pressing. If you have already collected the money, please send it to Hong Kong immediately. If the funds are not ready, please take urgent measures to help meet the needs. It is imperative that we get the funding now, else it will be detrimental to the cause. Please help us out of this difficult situation.... Comrades in Southeast Asia and Hong Kong are at their wits end. You people are my only hope and I expect a lot from you. No matter how much you may be able to collect, please send it over immediately....

On October 16, 1910, Sun wrote the fourth letter, which was again addressed to "the president of the Tung Meng Hui, Kwok-ming and other comrades in Hilo." This was again a long letter of four pages. In this letter, Sun informed them of a plan to stage another uprising and said that there was a good chance of succeeding. However, at least 100,000 yuan was needed. He was hoping that comrades in Southeast Asia, the United States, and Hawaii would provide the main portion of the money and could help raise this amount within one or two months. In the letter, he also said that the people in China were up in arms and were determined to sacrifice for the revolution. Even the soldiers in the Manchu army were inclined to revolt and join the revolution. The only thing lacking was timely funding. He also said that in China, comrades were ready to sacrifice their lives, and he hoped comrades overseas would do their best to provide money within two months.[16]

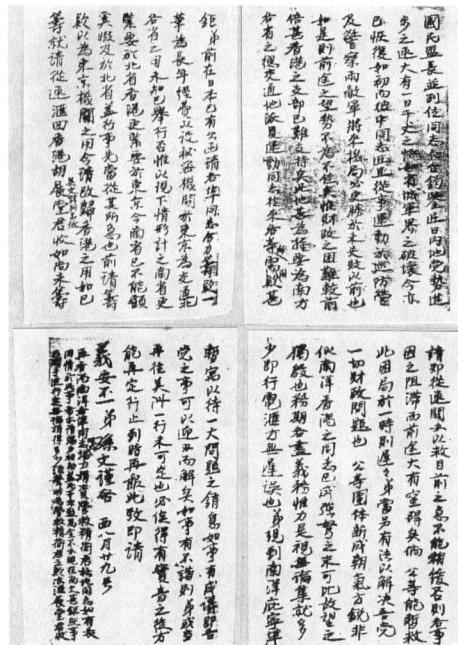

FIGURE 2.8. Letter of August 29 addressed to Kwok-ming (Lai Hip), written in Sun Yat-sen's handwriting. Reproduced courtesy of the Historical Commission of the Central Committee of the Chinese Kuomintang, Taipei, 1961.

The scheduled uprising mentioned in this letter was the famous Wong Fa Gong Uprising, which was launched on March 29, 1911. Unfortunately, this uprising failed again and seventy-two martyrs were killed.

Apparently, in 1910, the revolution was reaching a critical stage, and Sun was desperately in need of money. From these letters, one can see how he turned to his followers in Hawaii for help. He always had faith in the Chinese in Hawaii, and they surely did not disappoint him.

CONTRIBUTIONS OF THE CHINESE IN HILO

In the following year, 1911, Hilo members collected $5,000 and sent the money to Sun.[17] In March 1911, the Hilo members sent $3,000 Hong Kong dollars to the Revolutionary Army Headquarters in Hong Kong.[18]

By the turn of the century, the Chinese population on the island of Hawaii was at a peak, about 5,000 people, accounting for more than a fourth of all the Chinese then living in Hawaii.[19] Most of them were plantation workers or small merchants. Considering the population and the amount of donations they made, one can see that the Chinese in Hilo were truly enthusiastic and generous in contributing to the revolution the best they could.

In Hilo, Lai Hip (Kwok-ming), a well-known merchant, was a leader of the Chinese community. He met Sun in 1903 when Sun first visited Hilo. He became

SUN YAT-SEN'S FUND-RAISING IN HAWAII   53

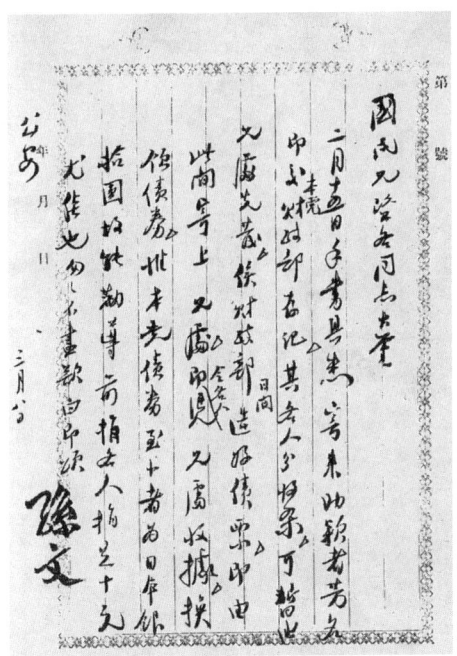

FIGURE 2.9. March 8 letter from Sun Yat-sen to Kwok-ming (Lai Hip) regarding the sale of Chinese Revolutionary Party bonds. Reproduced from the Lum Chee collection.

a staunch supporter of the revolution and a close friend of Sun. When Sun visited Hilo, he often stayed in Lai Hip's home. After Sun Yat-sen left Hawaii, he wrote to Lai Hip many times. Lai Hip played an important role in organizing the Chinese in Hilo to support the revolution. Unfortunately, he was shot by a gunman and died in November of 1915.[20] A few months before he died, he was still working hard to sell Chinese Revolutionary Party bonds that Sun issued in 1915 in Japan. Sun wrote him a letter on March 8, 1915, on this matter. The letter reads:

> Dear Brother Kwok Ming and comrades, this is to acknowledge receipt of your letter of February 15 in which a name list of those who bought the Bonds was enclosed. The name list was forwarded to the Ministry of Finance and registered. Please issue a temporary receipt to those who bought the Bond. The Finance Ministry will issue the bonds which will be sent over to you as soon as they are ready. The minimum denomination of this Bond is ten Japanese Yen. It will be better if people could buy at least that amount. Regards, Sun Wen [signed]. Date: March 8.

The letter is not in Sun Yat-sen's handwriting, but Sun signed it. The date of the letter did not specify the year in which it was written. Since it refers to the bonds issued in the Japanese yen, it was probably written in 1915, the same year the bonds were issued. The bonds were dated May 10 and thus were issued after this letter was written.

From this letter, it can be seen that many Chinese in Hilo bought these bonds

FIGURE 2.10. The Chinese Revolutionary Party bond issued May 10, 1915. The text on the bond reads:
"Ten yen:
 "– payment and pay back are all in Japanese currency
 "– interest is one hundred percent
 "– to be repaid within three years after the establishment of the new government—after the Treasury Department announces repayment, bearer of the bond may receive the principal and interest from institutions set up for repayment of revolutionary debts or the Fund-Raising Bureau that sold the bonds
 "– the bond is transferable
"Date: May 10, 1915. [signature and chop] Sun Wen, Premier of the Chinese Revolutionary Party."
Reproduced from the Lum Chee collection.

as a list of the names of those who bought them was enclosed in the letter Lai Hip sent to Sun.

After Lai Hip died, Sun Yat-sen wrote two letters to comrades in Hilo. One was a letter of condolence to the family of Lai Hip and the Chinese Revolutionary Party branch in Hilo dated December 15, 1915. In the letter, Sun said that when

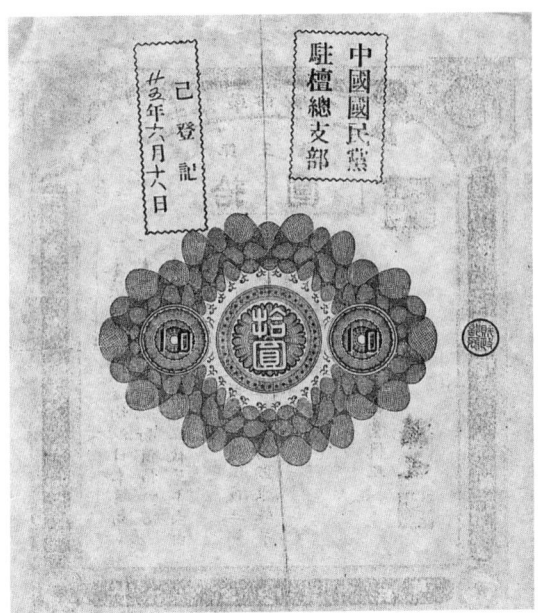

FIGURE 2.11. The reverse side of the May 10, 1915, Chinese Revolutionary Party bond in the Lum Chee collection bears two stamps. One says, "Registered, June 18, 1936." The other says, "Hawaii Branch of the Chinese Kuomintang." The stamps indicate that the bond was registered by the Honolulu office of the Kuomintang in 1936 for the purpose of repayment.

he heard the sad news of Lai Hip's death, he was so sorry and felt the pain and loss deeply. Sun said that Lai Hip worked hard for our country and never complained about the hardship and difficulties in his work. "We relied heavily on him to work for our party," Sun said. In this letter, Sun extended his deep condolences to the family, and he told the comrades to extend his many kind words he wanted to say to the family. The second was addressed to Wong Gum and dated January 16, 1916. Sun expressed his regret at not being able to attend the funeral of Lai Hip. Copies of the two letters are included in Appendix 10.

THE AMERICAN CHINESE REVOLUTIONARY ARMY FUND-RAISING BUREAU

Sun's most successful fund-raising operation was organizing the American Chinese Army Fund-Raising Bureau and the issuance of the gold dollar banknotes in July 1911. By that time, the revolution was gathering momentum. Revolutionary

FIGURE 2.12. The headquarters of the Chee Kung Tong at 36 Spofford Alley in San Francisco, photographed in 1998. The building still serves as the organization's headquarters. Photo by Wong Sze-kwong.

FIGURE 2.13. A plaque in Spofford Alley in San Francisco's Chinatown tells the story of Sun Yat-sen's using the Chee Kung Tong headquarters as his office when he visited San Francisco. Photo by Wong Sze-kwong.

spirits of people in China as well as overseas were soaring. People were confident that the revolution was going to succeed, and they were willing to give support, financially or otherwise. Fund-raising among the overseas Chinese became much easier than in earlier years.

In July 1911, when Sun was in San Francisco, he helped the Chee Kung Tong, also known as the Chinese Free Masons, a Chinese society with more than 100,000 members all over the United States, to revise its charter and by-laws to include the political platform of overthrowing the Manchus and establishing a republic in China. All the Tung Meng Hui members in the United States joined the Chee Kung Tong and the two organizations merged. To support the revolution, they jointly organized the American Chinese Revolutionary Army Fund-Raising Bureau. Because the Chee Kung Tong belonged to the Hoong Moon Fraternity, it was also called the Hoong Moon Fund-Raising Bureau. To get a tax exemption, the Bureau was registered with the U.S. government under the name Kwok Min Charity Bureau. Its office was located at 36 Spofford Alley in San Francisco's Chinatown, which was the headquarters of the Chee Kung Tong. Sun had his office here when he visited San Francisco.[21]

In Lum Chee's collection, there is a letter of September 4, 1911, written and signed by Sun, addressed to the "Comrades in Hilo." The letter was written on stationery printed with the letterhead of the Kwok Min Charity Bureau and the address was the same 36 Spofford Alley, San Francisco.

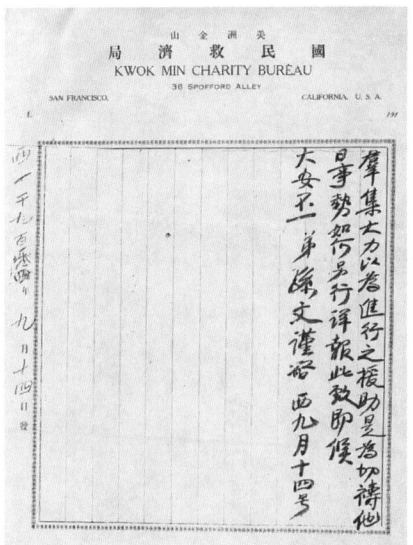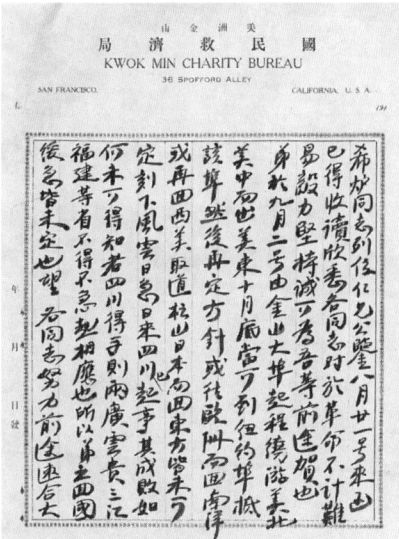

FIGURE 2.14. Letter of September 4, 1911, written and signed by Sun Yat-sen. Reproduced from the Lum Chee collection.

The letter was dated September 4 without specifying the year. Judging from the contents of this letter, it was probably written in September of 1911, one and a half month before the October 10th Wuchang Uprising. In the letter, Sun talked about the situation in China on the eve of the successful uprising and his own travel plans. In English translation, the letter reads:

> To the comrades in Hilo. Thanks for your letter of Aug. 31. I feel very encouraged to hear about your unswerving support to the revolution. I left San Francisco on Sept. 2 and proceeded to North America, the Midwest, and the East. I expect to arrive in New York and will make plans either to visit Europe first, then return to Southeast Asia, or to return to the West Coast, then go back to the East via Hawaii and Japan. I have not made any definite plans yet. However, there are signs of revolutionary disturbances in Szechuan Province. I don't know whether they have succeeded or not. If the uprising went well, then Kwangtung, Kwangsi, Yunan, Kweichow, and Fukien Provinces will follow. So my plans of going back home have not been determined. Hope all my comrades will work hard, unite, and support the revolution. Will write you later and report to you. Warm regards, Sun Wen [signed], Sept. 14.

After the Hoong Moon Fund-Raising Bureau was formed in San Francisco in July 1911, the gold dollar banknotes of "the Republic of China" were issued. At

FIGURE 2.15. Gold dollar bank note, one side printed in Chinese and the other in English. Reproduced from the Lum Chee collection.

SUN YAT-SEN'S FUND-RAISING IN HAWAII   59

FIGURE 2.16.   Reverse side of the gold dollar banknote, printed in English. Both sides contain the message, "Promises to pay the Bearer on its formation at the State Treasury or its Agents Abroad." The note carries the signatures of Sun Wen, premier of the Chinese Revolutionary Army, and Lee Gnong Hap, treasurer of the Chinese Revolutionary Army Fund-Raising Bureau. On these bonds are two stamps: "Registered, June 18, 1936" and "Hawaii Branch of the Kuomintang" (the same as in Fig. 2.11). Reproduced from the Lum Chee Collection.

the time of issuance, the Republic of China had not yet been established. Sun was confident, however, that the revolution would soon succeed and the republic would soon be established, so he issued the bonds in the name of the republic.

From July to September 1911, a total of US$144,130.41 was raised by selling gold dollar banknotes all over the world.[22] In Hilo alone, $5,000 worth of the banknotes were sold.[23] This fund was used to support the October 10th Wuchang Uprising, which finally overthrew the Manchu regime and established the Republic of China.

After the establishment of the Hoong Moon Fund-Raising Bureau, all donations from overseas Chinese were consolidated in this one institution. For example, in the Lum Chee collection, there is a letter dated September 13 that Sun sent to the Hilo comrades. In this letter, Sun requested that all donations be sent to the Fund-Raising Bureau in San Francisco.

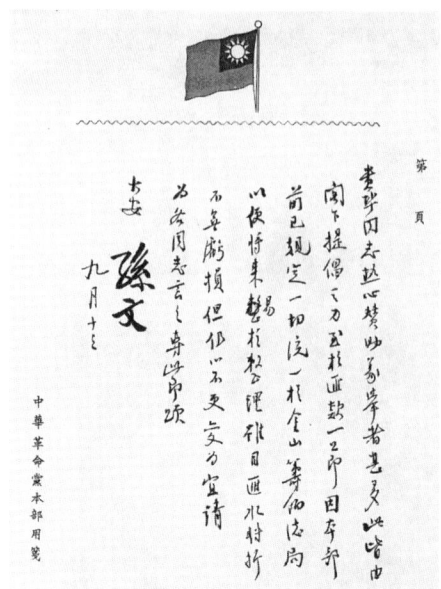

FIGURE 2.17. Letter of September 13 on Chinese Revolutionary Party stationery, signed by Sun Yat-sen. Reproduced from the Lum Chee collection.

The letter was written on the stationery of the Chinese Revolutionary Party with a flag of the Republic of China. This letter was signed by Sun Yat-sen but is not in his handwriting. Again the letter was dated September 13 without specifying the year in which it was written. According to Feng Tzu-yu, as early as 1911, Sun changed the name of Tung Meng Hui to Chinese Revolutionary Party when he was in San Francisco, although the Chinese Revolutionary Party was not officially formed in Tokyo until 1914.[24] Moreover, the letter refers to the Fund-Raising Bureau in San Francisco, which was formed in 1911, so most probably it was written in 1911.

The letter reads:

> There are so many members in Hilo who enthusiastically support the revolution. I sincerely appreciate it. As to sending over the money, it is advisable to consolidate and send the money to San Francisco Fund-Raising Bureau. Maybe it will cause some losses due to the exchange rate, but it will be easier to manage. Please explain to the comrades. Regards, Sun Wen [signed], September 13.

FUND-RAISING AFTER THE ESTABLISHMENT OF THE REPUBLIC

After the founding of the Republic of China, the political situation in China was chaotic. Warlords in different parts of the country seized power and waged wars against each other. Sun Yat-sen worked hard to unify China and institute a democratic government. All these years, he continued to solicit financial support from the overseas Chinese. The Chinese in Hawaii continued their support and donated even more money.

FIGURE 2.18. Receipt for a donation made by Lum Wai-cheng (Lum Chee) to the National Fund in 1912. The receipt reads: "This is to acknowledge receipt of donation of US$150.00 to the National Fund by Mr. Lum Wai-Cheng. [signed] Wong Gum, agent for the Fund. Anyone who collects money without giving a receipt is an imposter. Date: Nov. 21, 1912." Reproduced from the Lum Chee collection.

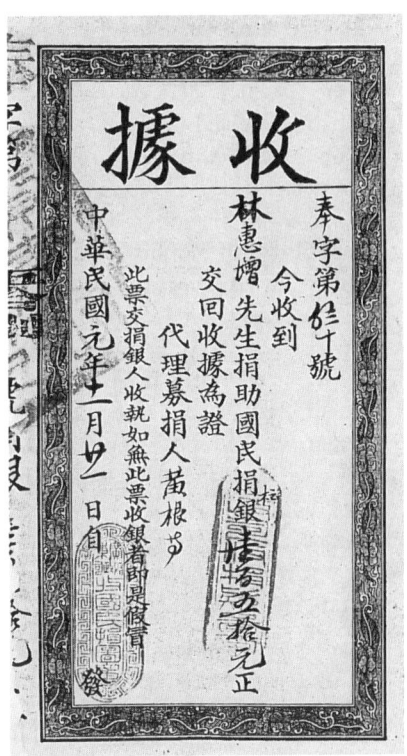

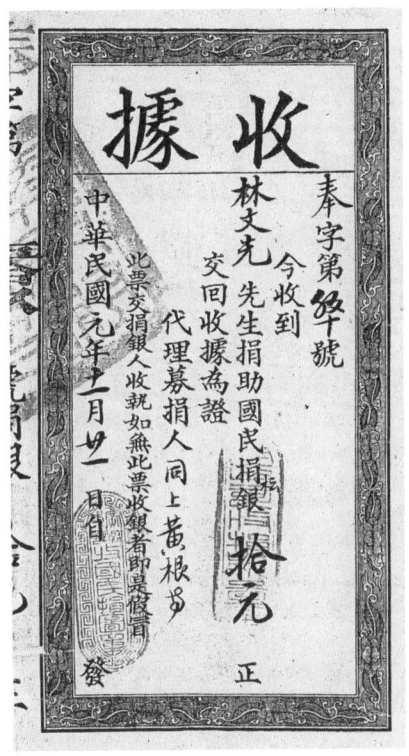

FIGURE 2.19. Receipt for a donation of US$10.00 to the National Fund made in the name of Lum Mun-kong (Raymond Lum). At the time, Lum was only eight months old. It was Chinese custom for parents to give a *lishee* (gift) to a child. In this case, the gift was a receipt for the donation. Reproduced from the Lum Chee collection.

According to Wen Phong-fei, after October 10, 1911, the Chinese in Honolulu were so concerned about what was happening in China that many people swarmed into the *Chee Yow Shin Bo* office every day to ask for news. Once in a while, the newspaper received newsletters from Hong Kong carrying news about the latest developments. There were so much conflicting news, however, that the Tung Meng Hui members decided to send Wen Phong-fei back to China to find out what the situation was. They gave him $1,000 for travel expenses. Wen arrived in China by the end of 1911 and found out that the revolutionary army was fighting against the warlords and was short of funds. He reported to the comrades in Honolulu, and in no time, he received a donation of US$20,000, which he forwarded to the Revolutionary Army Headquarters in Nanking.[25] At that time, Nanking was the capital of the newly formed republic.

In 1912, a National Fund-Raising Bureau was established in Honolulu. The chairman was Young Kwong-tat, the vice-chairman was Lee Dat-yip, the treasurer was Young Ahin, the secretary was Young Hook-ing, and the auditors were C. K. Ai and Yan Sen.[26] In Lum Chee's collection, there are two receipts for his donations to this fund. Wong Gum's name was written on the receipt as the agent for the fund. Wong Gum was the same person who, together with Lai Hip, welcomed Sun Yat-sen and accompanied him to Hilo in 1903.

ACCOUNTING FOR THE FUNDS RAISED

A question arises as to whether the funds Sun Yat-sen raised were accounted for. The answer is a definite yes. As early as 1909, a man named Tao Cheng-chang spread rumors that Sun was "pocketing the money he raised." Such slander was very detrimental to Sun's reputation and fund-raising efforts, so he was obliged to respond. In a letter written in October 1909 and addressed to his friend Wu Jing-heng, Sun gave a detailed accounting of the expenses of the uprising and of the funds he raised from overseas Chinese all over the world.[27] The letter was published in the French magazine *The New Century*, in the Chinese newspapers in San Francisco and Vancouver, and in the *Chee Yow Shin Bo* in Honolulu.[28]

Sun fought back with solid facts and shattered his enemies' slanders. Sun's enemies viciously tried to sabotage his fund-raising efforts but inadvertently did a favor for historians because Sun's letter serves as precious documentation of the fund-raising aspects of the ten uprisings. Very detailed accounts of fund-raising were kept, as is shown in the article written by Jiang Yung-jing, "The Study of the Funding of the Ten Uprisings Before the Hsin Hai Revolution."[29]

During his more than sixteen years of exile, Sun relied on his friends' financial support. In an interview with a reporter from the Australian monthly *Progress* in 1912, after he resigned his presidency, he said:

> Friends provided me with funds, and here I must mention the constant fidelity of well-wishers to the great cause I have all these years endeavored to promote. They have never

failed me. But then, fortunately, apart from travelling, my wants are few. I have often for weeks lived on a little rice and water....[30]

Here was this great revolutionary, dedicating his whole life to the Chinese people, yet living on a little rice and water for weeks. One could not refrain paying respect to this great man.

Friends who knew Sun well had many stories to tell about how frugal he was in his lifestyle. In Hsiang Ting-yung's book, *The Founding Father's Seven Visits to the United States and Hawaii*, there is, for example, a story about Sun's life in New York's Chinatown. For his meals, Sun used to go to a restaurant located at Mott Street and Doyers Street owned by a lady whose name was "Number two sister-in-law, Wong Er-sao." She was a staunch supporter of the revolution and was one of the few women who joined the Tung Meng Hui in 1909. When Sun went to have meals in her restaurant, she never charged him anything. Sun always ate one bowl of noodles, and Wong would offer more. But Sun always refused, saying he had had enough. So Wong changed the name of her restaurant to Yat Go Mien, which meant, a bowl of noodles. Wong Er-sao later sold the business, but the new owner kept the same name for the restaurant, which was in existence for more than seventy years before closing a few years ago.[31]

Sun also admitted in his interview with the Australian magazine *Progress*: "At other times, I have had difficulty in refusing the large sums placed at my disposal for some of my countrymen in America are very rich, generous and patriotic."

Although Sun handled large sums, he never squandered any money on his own personal expenses. Even for the support of his family, he had to ask his brother and friends for help. His family lived in Maui with his brother Sun Mei, who had been taking care of his family all along. Pang Hong-kwun, whose grandfather, Chang Keong, was Sun Mei's business partner and lived on Sun Mei Kula ranch during the early 1900s, recalled that her mother used to tell stories of Sun Yat-sen's family. According to one story, Sun had no money to send to his family, and his first wife, Loo Mu-chun, had to raise chickens to earn some income.[32]

After Sun Mei filed bankruptcy and left Hawaii in 1907, Sun's family moved to Penang in the Malay Peninsula. Sun's Chinese friends in Penang took turns taking care of the family. In a letter written to his friend Deng Ze-ru in Siam (now Thailand) on July 18, 1911, Sun talked about the financial difficulties his family had to go through. He wrote:

> Now my family lives in Penang and the comrades there provide a hundred dollars for their living expenses every month. My two daughters are in school and when my wife gets sick, it is very hard for her to pay the medical expenses. It is true that it is hard to support a poor man for any length of time. They have already helped for more than six months. I would like to ask you, if I may, to get together ten or twenty friends, and ask each of them to provide five or ten dollars monthly to help my family in Penang. I would appreciate it if this can be arranged....[33]

From this letter, one can see what hardships Sun and his family had to suffer during those years. Sun Yat-sen's son, Sun Fo, did not go to Penang. He stayed in Honolulu and studied at St. Louis High School, and his educational expenses were provided by some of Sun's Chinese friends in Hawaii.[34]

REPAYMENT OF THE BONDS

After the establishment of the Republic of China, did Sun and his government honor their promises to redeem the bonds he had issued? During 1935 and 1936, the Kuomintang headquarters in Nanking had set up the Committee to Investigate the Debts of the Hsin Hai Revolution. One of the persons in charge was Lee Gnong-hap, who was the treasurer of the Hoong Moon Fund-Raising Bureau in San Francisco in 1911 and whose signature was on the gold dollar banknotes. He returned to China after 1912.[35]

On the gold dollar banknotes and other bonds that Lum Chee kept, there are stamps reading "Registered, June 18, 1936" and "The Hawaii Branch of the Chinese Kuomintang" (see Fig. 2.8). This is proof that bonds sold in Hawaii were registered and that the government intended to repay the buyers. But Lum Chee never cashed his bonds. He kept the originals of all the bonds he bought. C. K. Ai, on the other hand, claimed that he got his money back. He said in his biography, *My Seventy Nine Years in Hawaii,* "I bought two fifty dollars bonds which I gave my wife for safe keeping. After the Manchus were overthrown, the new Republic of China honored these bonds that were issued by Dr. Sun at a thousand dollars each."[36]

There may be others who were also repaid. However, there were some who were not paid back, either because they did not expect to be repaid or they were afraid of incrimination and had destroyed the bonds.

Monetary repayment was not the only thing Sun and the government did to acknowledge appreciation for those who rendered support to the revolution. Shortly after Sun was sworn in as the first president of the Republic of China in January 1912, he expressed his thanks to those who had supported the revolution by awarding citations and medals. For example, he sent three citations to people in Hawaii in 1912: one to Leong Hoy, the first president of the Tung Meng Hui; one to Zane Chong-fook, who donated generously to the *Chee Yow Shin Bo* and to the Wah Mun School (now Chung Shan School); and another to the newspaper *Chee Yow Shin Bo.*[37]

In the following years, Sun awarded silver medals of the second and third class to the following people on Maui to thank them for their support: Chock Cheong, Lau Ping, Dang Ming-san, Dan Siang, Tam Chi, Luke Chin, Tam Cheong, Dang Hu, and Yap Chau.[38]

Medals of the sixth class, issued by the Ministry of Finance of the Republic of China Government, were awarded to people who had made monetary donations.[39]

Sun Yat-sen always remembered those that had helped him. One example was Francis W. Damon (1852–1915). Damon was a writer, missionary, and builder of

FIGURE 2.20. Medal of the sixth class awarded by the Republic of China government to Loo Yuen Aiona, who frequently donated to the revolution. The medal is in the possession of Loo's daughter-in-law, Ngan-sum Loo (Summie Lum), who recalled that Loo received more than one medal and said her sons and grandsons played with them. The medal pictured here, photographed in 1998, is the only one left. Photo courtesy of Ngan-sum Loo.

FIGURE 2.21. Writer and missionary Francis W. Damon established himself as a friend of Hawaii's Chinese community in his work as superintendent of Chinese mission work for the Hawaiian Evangelical Association. Photo courtesy of the Hawaiian Mission Children's Society Library.

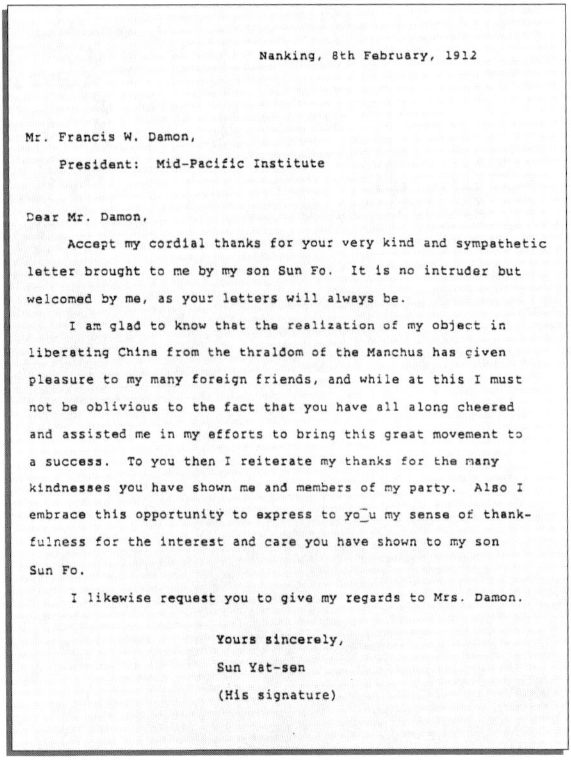

> Nanking, 8th February, 1912
>
> Mr. Francis W. Damon,
>   President: Mid-Pacific Institute
>
> Dear Mr. Damon,
>
>   Accept my cordial thanks for your very kind and sympathetic letter brought to me by my son Sun Fo. It is no intruder but welcomed by me, as your letters will always be.
>
>   I am glad to know that the realization of my object in liberating China from the thraldom of the Manchus has given pleasure to my many foreign friends, and while at this I must not be oblivious to the fact that you have all along cheered and assisted me in my efforts to bring this great movement to a success. To you then I reiterate my thanks for the many kindnesses you have shown me and members of my party. Also I embrace this opportunity to express to you my sense of thankfulness for the interest and care you have shown to my son Sun Fo.
>
>   I likewise request you to give my regards to Mrs. Damon.
>
>   Yours sincerely,
>   Sun Yat-sen
>   (His signature)

FIGURE 2.22. Sun Yat-sen's letter of February 8, 1912, to Francis W. Damon. Reproduced courtesy of C. F. Damon, Jr.

public service institutions and had been to Canton. It was as a missionary to the Chinese in Hawaii that he distinguished himself. He was superintendent of Chinese mission work for the Hawaiian Evangelical Association from 1881 and was also known as a friend of the Chinese community in Hawaii. He was a lifelong friend and supporter of Sun and the Chinese revolution. On February 8, 1912, Sun wrote in a letter of thanks: "[Y]ou have all along cheered and assisted me in my efforts to bring this great movement to a success. To you I reiterate my thanks and for the many kindnesses you have shown me and members of my party."[40] The original letter written by Sun Yat-sen is kept by the Damons as a family treasure.

Damon's grandson, C. F. Damon, Jr., is an attorney in Honolulu and is one of the directors of the Dr. Sun Yat-sen Hawaii Foundation in Honolulu.

THREE

Sun Yat-sen's Supporters in Hawaii

Sun Yat sen's supporters in Hawaii numbered in the thousands. Some were his family members, some his close friends. Most of them were members of the revolutionary organizations Sun founded. These organizations included:

Hsing Chung Hui 興中會 (Revive China Society), 1894;
Chung Hua Keming Jun 中華革命軍 (Chinese Revolutionary Army), 1903–1904;
Tung Meng Hui 同盟會 (Alliance Society), 1910;
Kuomintang 國民黨 (Nationalist Party), 1912;
Chung Hua Keming Tang 中華革命黨 (Chinese Revolutionary Party), 1914;
Chungkuo Kuomintang 中國國民黨 (Chinese Nationalist Party), 1917.

When the Hsing Chung Hui was first founded in Hawaii, 112 members were listed in the organization's ledger of members and dates of payment of membership dues kept by Ho Fon (Appendix 4). In his book *The Unofficial History of the Revolution,* Feng Tzu-yu listed the names of 138 Chinese of Hawaii (including Sun Yat-sen) who joined the Hsing Chung Hui.[1] According to Feng, during the seven years from 1894 to 1901, Hsing Chung Hui membership in China and all over the world, including Hawaii, Japan, Hong Kong, and South Africa, totaled a little more than five hundred.[2] The 138 members in Hawaii thus accounted for almost one-fifth of the total membership.

The Tung Meng Hui was a secret organization first founded in 1905 in Tokyo by merging the Hsing Chung Hui and other organizations. It was reorganized into the Kuomintang in 1912. Within the first year (1905–1906) after it was formed, the total membership developed to around ten thousand, including members in China and all over the world.[3] When the Tung Meng Hui was organized in Hawaii in 1910, one thousand or so members joined.[4] These figures alone show the important historical role the Chinese in Hawaii played in the revolution to establish a modern China.

In this chapter, some of the Chinese in Hawaii who joined the Hsing Chung

Hui and the Tung Meng Hui are identified and short biographical sketches are provided. We managed to collect information on thirty-four Hsing Chung Hui members and thirty-two Tung Meng Hui members. Of the thirty-four Hsing Chung Hui members, ten later became members of the Tung Meng Hui; they are not repeated among the thirty-two Tung Meng Hui members listed below. Because of the difficulties of collecting information, we cannot give full biographical sketches for each and every one of them.[5]

The persons discussed here, of course, constitute only a small fraction of the members of the organizations in Hawaii. Most were unsung heroes. Because people who joined these organizations risked being persecuted by the Manchu regime, many activities were kept secret. Some information was even kept from their family members or was destroyed to protect family members in China from persecution. For example, Hee Jack-son once had a picture taken with Sun Yat-sen together with Ching Wai-nam, Chang Kim, and Lee Chong. The Manchu consul got hold of a copy of the photo, and Hee had to hide and change his name.[6] Chang Kim's relatives in China were persecuted.[7] When other people heard such news, they destroyed whatever papers they had. Ching Chow burned the letters that Sun Yat-sen wrote to him after reading them.[8] Moreover, as time went by, older generations passed away and with them, a lot of information was lost. Thanks to researchers who had the foresight to collect and preserve information about the early supporters, it was possible to put together the information that follows. People who contributed to the cause of the revolution, whether or not their names are mentioned below, will always be remembered.

HSING CHUNG HUI MEMBERS WHO ATTENDED THE FIRST MEETING

The first meeting of the Hsing Chung Hui was held on November 24, 1894. Information on eighteen of the twenty-odd members who attended that meeting is given below.

Lau Cheong 劉祥 (Dates unknown)

Lau Cheong was the owner of the Wing Wo Tai store in Honolulu's Chinatown. He joined the Hsing Chung Hui and was elected president at the first meeting. Later, he was not active and ceased being the president.[9]

Wong Wah-fei 黃華恢 (Dates unknown)

Wong Wah-fei was an employee working in Lau Cheong's store, Wing Wo Tai. At the first meeting of the Hsing Chung Hui, he was elected treasurer. Later, he left Hawaii and moved to Mexico. In 1928, he went back to Shanghai and worked in the Shanghai Sun Sun Department Store.[10]

Ho Fon 何寬 (1861–1931)

Ho Fon was born in Chung Shan Country and came to Hawaii when he was seventeen years old. The ship he was on was shipwrecked off Molokai, and a part-Hawaiian sailor named Clarence Crabbe, Sr., helped him swim to shore. Ho Fon lived with him for a while and later went to school in Honolulu. He graduated from the Fort Street English School. Later he worked for thirty-two years in the Bank of Bishop and Company, Ltd., in Honolulu before he retired in 1929. Ho Fon was a close friend of C. K. Ai, who was Sun Yat-sen's classmate, and also became a close friend of Sun. The first Hsing Chung Hui meeting was held in his home located on Emma Lane in Honolulu, and he was elected one of the vice-chairmen at the meeting. After Lau Cheong resigned the chairmanship, Ho became chairman. He was also the editor of the *Tan San Sun Bo*, the official newspaper of the Hsing Chung Hui. The Hsing Chung Hui ledger of members and dates of payments of membership fees was in his safekeeping for thirty years.[11]

Ho Fon's great-grandson, K. Russell Ho, is a securities investigator for the State of Hawaii and volunteer photographer for the Dr. Sun Yat-sen Hawaii Foundation.

Ching Wai-nam 程蔚南 (Dates unknown)

Ching Wai-nam was a merchant in Honolulu and a relative of Sun Yat-sen. At the first meeting, he was elected secretary of the Hsing Chung Hui. He was the owner of the *Loong Kee Sun Bo*, which was formed in 1883 and carried only business news. In 1903, the newspaper was reorganized into the *Tan San Sun Bo*, the official newspaper of the Hsing Chung Hui, and played an important role in publishing articles explaining Sun Yat-sen's political views against those of the Bao Wong Hui.[12]

Hee Jack-son (Hee Chih-chen) 許直臣 (1867–1949)

Hee Jack-son was a founding member of the Hsing Chung Hui and was elected deputy secretary at the first meeting in 1894. He became Sun's right-hand man and drafted many documents. When Sun visited Hawaii, Hee spent a lot of time with him. Hee's son, Hon-chew, the famous artist, told the story that Hee went to Sun Mei's Kula ranch to visit Sun for three days. He did not even return home the day Hon-chew was born. Hee and Sun always discussed issues of the revolution all night long.

Hee Jack-son was born in Pan Sha, Chung Shan County. He came from a prominent family of the district. His father, Hee Chiung-chang, was a student of the Imperial Academy and superintendent of education in the Chung Shan County. Hee Jack-son was well educated in the Chinese classics.

Hee came to Hawaii in 1891. He went to Molokai, where he spent several months among the Hawaiians and learned to speak Hawaiian. The same year, he attended the coronation of Queen Liliuokalani as the representative of the Chinese community. The queen was so impressed with him that she sent him to the Royal School to study. Hee mastered the Hawaiian language and became a fluent interpreter. He set up Chinese language schools in Honolulu and on the outer islands. Many students attended his schools. In 1922, Hee went back to China at the request of Sun. For many years, he was in charge of Chung Shan County and served as mayor of Hua Hsian. He died in Hong Kong in 1949.[13]

LEE CHONG 李昌 (1851–1912)

Lee Chong's grandfather, Lee Say-duck, was a Taiping Rebellion leader and a Christian minister. His father, Lee Cheng-kao, was a Christian and also a rebel. Being constantly hunted by the Manchu regime, Lee Cheng-kao fled to Hong Kong, where Lee Chong received a fine education in both Chinese and English. He came to Hawaii in 1882 and worked as an interpreter in the Hawaiian legislature. He was elected one of the trustees of the Hsing Chung Hui at the first meeting. He and Soong Kee-yun went to Maui to talk to Sun Mei and formed the Maui chapter. He also worked as editor of the newspaper *Chee Yow Shin Bo*. Lee kept his attachment to Sun a secret, for his position enabled him to help Sun conceal his activities and avoid police surveillance.[14] Lee Chong retired to Hong Kong in 1909 and died there in 1912.[15]

CHANG KIM 鄭金 (1865–1914)

Chang Kim was a good friend of Sun Yat-sen and, together with his brother Chang Chau, was a sworn brother of Sun. When Sun was studying at Iolani School, he would spend weekends at Chang Kim's home at 146 Christley Lane. Chang Kim's mother was very kind to Sun and always did his laundry for him.[16]

In 1894, Chang Kim attended the first meeting of the Hsing Chung Hui and was elected one of the trustees. He was one of those who took part in military drill at the Mills School. In 1895, Chang Kim went with a group of other people to Canton and joined the first uprising. Chang Kim worked with the law firm Ashford and Ashford. In 1908, he assisted Mrs. Sun Mei in selling the Kula ranch assets to A. F. Tavares of Makawao, Maui.[17]

LEE TO-MA 李多馬 (1850–?)

Lee To-ma attended the first meeting of the Hsing Chung Hui and was elected one of the trustees at the meeting. He immigrated to Hawaii in 1880, settled on

Maui, and became a middleman for Kula farmers, carting produce from upcountry to the wharf in Kahului for shipment to Honolulu. By 1893, he moved to Honolulu, started a small business in general merchandise in Chinatown, and prospered. He was one of the few who contributed $100 to buy bonds issued by the Hsing Chung Hui in 1894.[18]

LUM KAM-CHIN 林鑑泉 (Dates unknown)

Lum Kam-chin was a newspaperman. He was assistant to Ching Wai-nam at *Loong Kee Sun Bo*. He attended the first meeting of the Hsing Chung Hui in 1894 and was elected one of the trustees. Later, he became the editor of the reorganized *Tan San Sun Bo*.[19]

C. K. AI (Chung Kun Ai) 鍾工宇 (1865–1961)

C. K. Ai, the founder of the City Mill Company, Ltd., was a classmate of Sun Yat-sen at Iolani School in 1879, and they became lifelong friends. During one Chinese New Year vacation, Ai was invited to stay with Sun in Sun Mei's store as Ai's parents were living in Kailua, Hawaii. In 1885, during Sun's second visit to Hawaii, he came to Honolulu penniless, and C. K. Ai helped him by donating his monthly salary to Sun. Ai was one of the twenty-odd people who attended the first meeting of the Hsing Chung Hui and later joined the Tung Meng Hui. He consistently supported the newspaper *Chee Yow Shin Bo* and the Chung Shan School in Honolulu. In his autobiography, he said:

> Once Sun brought along five hundred dollars worth of silk goods and asked me to sell for him. Within a very short time I was able to turn the cash over to him. He was greatly surprised and thanked me effusively. . . . He also mentioned that the money went to friends of the (revolutionary) movement.

Ai also wrote: "I had assured him time and again that should he need money, he was not to hesitate to call on me. He never asked me for direct financial contributions."

Ai had many reunions with Sun. In 1899, he visited Sun in Hong Kong. In 1913, he met Sun again in Tokyo and together they visited the Mitsubishi Company. Then they boarded the *Tenyo Maru* to return to Shanghai.[20]

Steven Ai, C. K. Ai's grandson, is one of the directors of the Dr. Sun Yat-sen Hawaii Foundation.

CHING NAM 陳南 (Dates unknown)

Ching Nam was a worker in Honolulu. He attended the first meeting of the Hsing Chung Hui and paid membership dues in April 1895. He returned to China and participated in the First Canton Uprising. After that, he worked at the *China Daily* of Hong Kong. A few years later, he passed away.[21]

Chang Chau 鄭照 (1870–1959)

Chang Chau, also known as Samuel Chang Chau, was Chang Kim's younger brother. He was born in Kohala, Hawaii, and was graduated from the Punahou Preparatory School in 1893. Chang Chau worked as an interpreter in the Honolulu District Court.

During Sun Yat-sen's fourth visit to Hawaii in 1903, he stayed in Chang Chau's home, located at 473 Kauluwela Lane.[22] Chang Chau was a sworn brother of Sun and was very loyal to him. When Sun was in Honolulu, Chang followed him around as a bodyguard. The family kept the pistol he used in defense of Sun and himself. He attended the first meeting of the Hsing Chung Hui.

In 1907, Chang was called by Sun to join an uprising in China. Later, he gave an interview to the *Star-Bulletin* in Honolulu in which he said: "In 1907, we tried again and we failed. . . . We were hounded like fleas. We went for days with nothing more to eat than a handful of rice. It was one long masquerade. . . . We had to keep changing our location and our costume. One of our many disguises was as beggars."

Chang Chau managed to escape and returned to Hawaii. When Sun Yat-sen became president, Chang went to Shanghai and worked as a commissioner of the Central Bank of China. Later, he returned to Honolulu to resume his position as court interpreter.[23] He was a Tung Meng Hui member in 1910.

Chock Hoy 卓海 (1863–?)

Chock Hoy was a native of Goon Tong village, Chung Shan Dictrict, and came to Hawaii in 1880. He began as a pharmacist and later was one of the founders of the Chinese American Bank. He also worked as an interpreter at the Immigration Station in Honolulu for twelve years. He was present at the first meeting of the Hsing Chung Hui and paid his membership dues on April 17, 1895. His name appears twice in the ledger of members and payment of membership dues.[24]

How Ai-chin 侯艾泉 (Dates unknown)

How Ai-chin was a worker in Honolulu. He attended the first meeting of the Hsing Chung Hui. In 1895, he went back to China with Sun Yat-sen and participated in the First Canton Uprising. After the failure of the uprising, he was included in the same "Wanted List" of the Kwangtung prosecutor in which Sun Yat-sen's name appeared. Those who apprehended him were promised an award of two hundred silver dollars while the award for Sun Yat-sen was one thousand silver dollars.[25]

HA PARK-CHEE 夏百子 (Ha Ah-park 夏亞伯) (Dates unknown)

Ha Park-chee was a native of Sun Hui. He attended the first meeting of the Hsing Chung Hui and followed Sun Yat-sen back to China to take part in the First Canton Uprising. After the uprising failed, he was on the wanted list of the Manchu government on which Sun Yat-sen's name appeared. The reward for capturing him was one hundred silver dollars. He managed to escape to Hong Kong together with Sun Yat-sen, carrying two pistols to protect Sun. Later he returned to Hawaii, and after 1911, he worked in Kwangtung government agencies.[26]

CHUNG MOOK-HEEN (H. A. Heen) 鍾木賢 (?–1922)

Chung Mook-heen had many other names, such as Chung Kwock-chee 鍾國柱 and Chung Sui-yong 鍾水養. He was naturalized under the name Harry A. Heen, and his descendants are identified by the surname Heen.

Chung Mook-heen attended the first meeting of the Hsing Chung Hui and was also the president of the Ket On Society in Honolulu. Chung was a supporter of Sun Yat-sen. When Sun joined the Ket On Society, it was Chung who sponsored him and convinced the other members to accept Sun into the Society. In the Ket On Society records, his name was Chung Kwock-chee.

Chung Mook-heen was a native of Wu Hua, West River, in Kwangtung Province. He came to Hawaii when he was seventeen years old and farmed on Maui. Later he became an enterprising merchant, and his business and real estate expanded to Maui, Kauai, and Oahu. He became one of the wealthiest leaders of the Chinese community. He married Mary Meheula, a descendant of a Maui *alii* who owned vast lands in Lahaina and Kaanapali. Mary died in 1902.

Chung sent his eldest son, Harry, back to China to establish continuity in the Chung genealogical line. After he returned to China, he took a Chinese name, Wun Cheong.

Chung returned to his native village in 1914. His son Ernest went with him to China. Ernest returned to Hawaii, but Chung Mook-heen decided to spend the rest of his days in his native village. He died in 1922.[27] He has many descendants in Hawaii, including Senator William H. Heen and Judge Walter M. Heen, his grandson.

LEE KAI 李杞 (Dates unknown)

Lee Kai was a worker in Honolulu. He attended the first meeting of the Hsing Chung Hui and later followed Sun Yat-sen back to China and took part in the First Canton Uprising.[28]

Soong Kee-yun 宋居仁 (1854–1937)

Soong Kee-yun came from Chih Pu village, Hua Hsian, Kwangtung Province. He came to Honolulu in 1881 and opened a small restaurant. When Sun Yat-sen came to Hawaii in 1885, he lived in a room on the second floor of a Chinese herb store neighboring Soong's restaurant. Sun had his meals there, so the two became friends and talked about the need for change in China. When the Hsing Chung Hui was founded in 1894, Soong was one of the first to join and attended the first meeting. Soon after, he closed his business and devoted all his energies to the cause of the revolution. He established a meeting place for Hsing Chung Hui members on the second floor of the Chinese Fire Station, which was located on the northwest corner of Maunakea and Pauahi Streets. He and Lee Chong went to Kahului to form the Hsing Chung Hui Maui chapter.

In 1895, Soong followed Sun to Hong Kong and participated in many revolutionary activities. After the success of the Wuchang Uprising, Soong returned to farming in Hua Hsian. He died in 1937 with hardly anything left for his family. At his funeral, a booklet was published to commemorate him. In this booklet, he was quoted as saying: "Empty handed I come to this world, and empty handed I go."

Soong Kee-yun married a Hawaiian woman, a sister of Robert William Wilcox. They had two sons, Soong Shao-kwai and Soong Shao-yim. After Mrs. Soong died in 1889, Soong took his two sons back to China.

Soong Shao-kwai was born in 1882 in Hawaii but grew up in Canton, where he attended a military school. He joined the revolutionary army and became a colonel. In 1914, when he was in Hong Kong, he wrote an article opposing Yuan Shih-kai, and under pressure from Yuan's men, he was arrested. Only through the good offices of the American consul-general was he allowed to return to Honolulu. His story was reported in the *Pacific Commercial Advertiser* in Honolulu on April 18, 1915. Later, he went back to China again and joined in the war against Yuan Shih-kai. His army was defeated and he was killed.

Soong Shao-yim was a pilot. In 1921, he was assistant to the chief of the anti-smuggling patrol. In 1924, he was killed in an ambush. Hawaiian blood was shed for the revolution to establish a modern China.[29]

OTHERS WHO JOINED THE HSING CHUNG HUI AFTER THE FIRST MEETING

Zane Chong-fook 曾長福 (Dates unknown)

Zane Chong-fook was a wealthy merchant in Honolulu. He joined the Hsing Chung Hui in 1903. In 1907, he took over the *Tan San Sun Bo* when Ching Wei-nam could not support the newspaper financially and changed its name to *Ming Sun Yat Bo*. One year later, the paper again changed its name to *Chee Yow Shin Bo*.

He gave generous financial support to the paper. He joined the Tung Meng Hui in 1910 and was one of the most active members in the organization. He was also a big donor to the Wah Mun School.[30] In 1917, he returned to China and invested in there. Later, he worked in Nanking and Shanghai.[31]

YOUNG MUN-NAP 楊文納 (Dates unknown)

Young Mun-nap was Sun Yat-sen's uncle, the brother of Sun's mother. He was a businessman in Honolulu and brought Sun Mei to Honolulu. He paid Hsing Chung Hui membership dues in January 1895. He advised Sun to join the Ket On Society and was one of those who played a role in acquiring a Territory of Hawaii birth certificate for Sun Yat-sen.[32]

LUKE CHAN 陸燦 (Luke Mun-chan 陸文燦) (1874–1952)

Luke Chan was born in Choy Hang, the same village where Sun Yat-sen was born. A boyhood friend of Sun, he came to Hawaii in 1887. He was probably the first student of Chinese ancestry to graduate from Punahou School. Later, he joined the fledgling H. Hackfeld & Company, which was to become American Factors. He began as a salesman and retired as manager of the American Factors dry goods department in 1942.

He was the founder of the Chinese-English Debating Society and served six terms as president. This Society was most active in support of Sun's revolutionary movement. Luke was the editor-in-chief of the *Tan San Sun Bo,* which publicized Sun's revolutionary ideas. In 1896, after the First Canton Uprising failed, he helped to bring Sun's family members to Hawaii to escape persecution. He joined the Hsing Chung Hui in 1894.[33]

Luke Chan was an energetic, respected leader in the Honolulu Chinese community. He was a founder of the See Dai Doo Society and served ten terms as president. He was also active in charities. Luke Chan's uncle was Lu How-tung, Sun's childhood friend. Lu How-tung and Sun together instigated the First Canton Uprising. Unfortunately, Lu How-tung was arrested and executed. He was one of the first martyrs who sacrificed their lives for the revolution.[34]

Carolyn Luke, maternal granddaughter of Luke Chan, is one of the directors of the Dr. Sun Yat-sen Hawaii Foundation in Honolulu.

KAN WING-CHEW 簡永照 (Dates unknown)

In the winter of 1895, after the First Canton Uprising failed, Sun Yat-sen returned to Hawaii. Together with Sun Mei and the brothers Chang Kim and Chang Chau, Kan Wing-chew became a sworn brother of Sun.[35] He joined the Hsing Chung Hui and paid membership fees in April 1895 (Appendix 5).

Yap Kwai-fong 葉桂芳 (1873–1935)

Yap Kwai-fong joined the Hsing Chung Hui in December 1894. He was born in Honolulu and attended the Haleiwa Mission School from 1877 to 1879 and the Fort Street Chinese Church School from 1880 to 1886. He worked hard, taking on jobs from tailor's apprentice to interpreter. Beginning in 1899, he worked for the Bank of Hawaii for twenty-nine years, first as a collector and then as an assistant cashier.

Yap Kwai-fong was involved in numerous educational, civic, and religious projects throughout his life. He was very much interested in the educational problems of Hawaii. He rallied the support of people of all ranks in the society and handed the territorial legislature a petition with five hundred signatures urging the creation of a public university. Both houses unanimously passed the act establishing the University of Hawaii in 1919. Therefore he was known as the "Father of the University of Hawaii."

He was also the president of the Chinese-English Debating Society, which supported Sun Yat-sen in the early years. He was one of those who participated in military drill at the Mills School.[36]

Lee Kwong-fai 李光輝 (Dates unknown)

Lee Kwong-fai, according to his grandson, Frank Lee, in Honolulu, was a tailor. He paid his membership dues November 29, 1894, and joined the Hsing Chung Hui (Appendix 5). He was a member of the Chinese-English Debating Society, which supported Sun Yat-sen's activities, and most of the members of the Society joined the Hsing Chung Hui. The Society by-laws were so written that after a member died, his eldest son inherited his father's membership. Frank Lee is now the president of the Debating Society.[37]

HSING CHUNG HUI MEMBERS ON MAUI

Sun Mei 孫眉 (S. Ahmi) (1854–1914)

Sun Mei, Sun Yat-sen's older brother, was born in Choy Hang village and came to Hawaii in 1871. He started to work on a vegetable farm and then leased land in Ewa, Oahu, from the government to plant rice. By the time he was twenty-four years old, he went back to China to get married and at the same time, he recruited more than a hundred laborers to come to Hawaii. Soon after, he opened a store in Honolulu. As the sugar industry developed and the number of Chinese laborers on Maui grew, Sun Mei moved to Kahului in 1881 and opened a grocery store. His business expanded, and he leased land from the government to start a cattle ranch at Kula. He was a generous and hospitable host; people called him the "Maui King."

Sun Mei supported Sun Yat-sen's education, both in high school and in medical schools. Sun Mei was also a staunch supporter of the revolution. He practically gave all he had to support the revolution and exhausted his cash assets. In 1906, he filed for bankruptcy and went to live in Kowloon.

Sun Fo, Sun Yat-sen's son, said on October 4, 1971, in a speech to the Overseas Chinese Administration Institute of Taiwan, that whenever his father had a plan of action, he invariably turned to Sun Mei for money. The sum each time reached into the tens of thousands. Therefore six or seven years before 1911, Sun Mei was no longer in a position to support Sun Yat-sen financially.

In November 1911, Kwangtung Province was taken over by the revolutionary forces, and a group of Tung Meng Hui members and friends signed a petition asking Sun Yat-sen to nominate Sun Mei as governor of the province. Sun refused on the grounds that Sun Mei was good at business but not at politics. Sun Mei went to live in Macao and died in 1914.

Sun Mei's son, Sun Chong, studied medicine in California and returned to China to join the revolution after 1911. In 1917, he was assigned to the military headquarters in Canton. On one occasion when he was carrying the army payroll to Whampoo, he was drowned when the steamship he was in was hit by the enemy and capsized. The incident grieved Sun extremely, and at Sun Chong's funeral, he wrote a scroll: "Sacrificed for the country." The Military Government gave him the posthumous title of army colonel.[38]

DANG YUM-NAM 鄧蔭南 (1864–1923)

Dang Yum-nam, also known as Dang Soong-sing 鄧松盛 and Dang San-po 鄧三伯, was from Kai Ping District, Kwangtung Province, and was a member of the Triad, the secret society of the Hoong Moon Fraternity. The exact year of his coming to Hawaii is not known. His grandnephew, Dang Seck-yen, said that he came as a sugar-plantation laborer. Later he was promoted to foreman, and he became a shareholder in a grocery store in Kahului and a salt factory nearby.

After he joined the Hsing Chung Hui in Honolulu in 1894, he liquidated his personal assets and returned to China to join the revolution. He participated in and donated a large sum of money to buy weapons for the First Canton Uprising. In 1900, he fought in the Waichou Uprising. He was a loyal follower of Sun Yat-sen and took part in many revolutionary wars. Later, Dang went to Hong Kong and started a farm to take in comrades who had to flee the country because of Manchu persecution. In 1920, he was elected mayor of Kai Ping and for several years served as a good mayor. In 1923, he died in Macao.

Sun wrote an eulogy for Dang Yum-nam: "He loved his country all his life; he was loyal to the party; he had no time for his family; the older he became, the greater his integrity. As I behold his portrait, I fondly cherish the voice of my dear friend." He conferred on Dang the posthumous rank of army general. Dang's remains were removed from Macao and reburied in Canton in June of 1929. With funds donated by Chinese in Maui. A new marker was placed on his grave.³⁹

Lau Tang 劉登 (1877–1961)

Lau Tang was a native of Maui. He paid his Hsing Chung Hui membership dues in January 1895. Later, he moved to Honolulu and was president of Liberty Bank. He had a grocery store in Waianae, Oahu, known as the Lau Tang Store. He was also member and president of the Chinese-English Debating Society.⁴⁰

Lau Yo-ke 劉其玉 (1874–?)

Lau Yo-ke was a native of Cheong-kong village, Duck Doo, Chung Shan District. He came to Hawaii in 1894 and was a dry-goods and grocery merchant in Moanalua, Oahu. By 1936, he retired. He joined in the Hsing Chung Hui and later the Tung Meng Hui. He was active in various Chinese societies in Honolulu.⁴¹

MEMBERS OF THE CHUNG HUA KEMING JUN IN HILO, 1903–1904

Mao Man-ming 毛文明 (Dates unknown)

Mao Man-ming was a Christian minister in China. He first joined the Hsing Chung Hui in Canton in 1900. Another Hsing Chung Hui member in Canton, Shih Jian-ru, tried to install a bomb to kill the governor of Kwangtung. Shih was arrested and executed. Since Shih had stored his explosives in Mao Man Ming's home, Mao had to flee China and went to Hawaii in 1903. He continued to be a Christian minister in Hilo.

Mao invited Sun Yat-sen to visit Hilo and talk to the Chinese community. After Sun's visit, the Chung Hua Keming Jun was formed in Hilo. Mao introduced

Lai Hip and others to Sun Yat-sen. In 1907, Mao Man-ming was a teacher in the Mills Institute in Honolulu. He returned to China after 1911 and became the mayor of Lian County, where he had formerly been a Christian minister.⁴²

Lai Hip 黎協 (Lai Kwok-ming 黎國民) (1863–1915)

Lai Hip was born in China in November 1863. He came to Hawaii in 1875 and was first employed on a plantation on Molokai. Later he moved to Hilo. He worked as a plantation worker for eight years and accumulated enough money to start a small merchandise business in Hilo. His business grew into three or four general-merchandise stores. He also owned real estate and was interested in cane planting. He was a leader of the Chinese community and was well-known among other races in Hilo. He was also known for his generosity in supporting charities in the community.

When Sun Yat-sen visited Hilo in December 1903, Lai Hip and Wong Gum headed the welcoming committee and accompanied Sun by train from Ka'u to Hilo. He became a good friend of Sun and was one of the most enthusiastic supporters of the revolution. He was in charge of the Chung Hua Keming Jun in Hilo after it was formed in 1903. In 1910, he became the chairman of the Tung Meng Hui Hilo chapter, which had 385 members.⁴³

In 1910, Sun Yat-sen wrote four letters to "the comrades of Hawaii"; two of the four letters were addressed to "Kwok-ming and other comrades." "Kwok-ming" was Lai Hip's other name. In Lum Chee's collection, there is also one letter signed by Sun and addressed to "Brother Kwok-ming and other comrades." The contents of these letters are discussed in chapter 2 above.

Lai Hip married a part-Hawaiian woman and had ten sons and daughters. The only surviving child is Elizabeth Lai Hip Lum. There are many grandsons and granddaughters. According to one granddaughter, Muriel Lai Hip De Ponte, Lai Hip was killed because he was so dedicated to supporting the revolution that some people were jealous of him. Muriel De Ponte said that her father, Lai Hip's second son, Herbert Lai Hip, told her that there was someone who was behind the assailant who killed Lai Hip. ⁴⁴

After Lai Hip died, Sun Yat-sen felt it was a great loss and wrote a letter of condolence to the family and the Chinese Revolutionary Party branch of Hilo on December 14, 1915. In the letter, Sun said that he had heard that Lai Hip had been killed and "on hearing this sad news, I am terribly sorry and felt the loss deeply. Mr. Lai worked hard for our country and he never complained for the hardship and difficulties he had to go through. We relied a lot on him to work for our party...." In the letter Sun also said:

"Please extend my deep condolences and my many kind words to the family members of Mr. Lai Hip." On January 25, 1916, Sun Yat-sen wrote a letter in reply to Wong Gum and Lau Oh, who had written the letter that informed Sun of Lai Hip's funeral and also sent the funds they had raised for Sun Yat-sen in his fight against Yuan Shi-kai. In this letter, Sun said:

> When I heard the sad news that Mr. Lai Hip was assassinated, I was shocked and terribly sorry. I regretted deeply that I could not attend the memorial service and the funeral as I was many thousands of miles away from Hawaii. I trust you and others will continue on with the work that Mr. Lai Hip had dedicated to and could not have finished. Mr. Lai Hip in heaven would be happy to know that although he died, you were carrying on with his unfinished work. . . .

For the full text of the two letters, see Appendix 10.

WONG GUM (W. K. Akana) 黃根 (Dates unknown)

It is not known when Wong Gum first came to Hawaii. As early as 1888, he was listed in the *Husted's Directory of the Hawaiian Kingdom* as "W. K. Akana, Coffee Salon, Hilo." In 1890, his name appeared as "W. K. Akana, Bakery, Hilo" in the directory. The coffee shop and bakery had the same address. People gathered there to gossip and sometimes talked about politics. When Sun Yat-sen's political rival, Liang Chi-chao, went to Hilo, Wong Gum befriended him. But later, Wong became a follower of Sun. When Sun visited Hilo in 1903, he and Lai Hip were on the welcoming committee and accompanied Sun by train from Ka'u to Hilo. While in Hilo, Sun stayed in Wong Gum's home, which was located near the corner of Keawe and Haili Streets. Wong Gum finally returned to China in his old age and died there.

Wong Gum's name appears on the receipt for Lum Chee's donation to the National Fund in 1912. This shows he was active in supporting fund-raising activities in Hawaii.[45]

LUM CHEE 林志 (Lum Wai-cheng 林惠增) (1868–1941)

Lum Chee was born in Leong Doo, Chung Shan County. When he was sixteen years old, he came to Honolulu and was hired as a houseboy by a British judge. Later, he became a grocer in Honolulu's Chinatown. His store was burned down in the 1900 Chinatown fire, and he moved to Hilo, where he started a general merchandise store. He was able to read and write Chinese, so he helped many fellow Chinese write letters back to their families.[46]

When Sun Yat-sen visited Hilo in 1903, Lum Chee joined the Chung Hua Keming Jun in Hilo and became an active supporter of Sun. He bought military bonds many times and kept the originals of many of them. He kept a canceled check of 1904 that was endorsed by Sun as well as letters written or signed by Sun. Lum Chee had the foresight to keep all these important historical documents and before he died, he told his son Raymond to donate these historical documents to China.[47] In 1985, Raymond Lum went to Beijing and presented these documents to the Sun Yat-sen Society. The *People's Daily of China* reported the news in its August 26, 1985, issue. The originals of the documents are now kept in the Museum of the Chinese Revolution. In 1986, the Sun Yat-sen Society in Beijing published the book *Collection of Manuscripts of Sun Yat-sen—Letters*. Sun's letter of September 14, 1911, is reproduced in this collection.

Lum Chee later became a member of the Tung Meng Hui Hilo chapter. His membership card is shown in chapter 1.

Loo Akau 盧阿球 (盧扆球) (1888–1972)

Loo Akau was born in Hawaii and received his education at the old Mills School. He first worked as an apprentice and later started his own business. He became the proprietor and manager of the New Market in Hilo, dealing in foods, dry goods, and sundries. When Sun Yat-sen visited Hilo in 1903 and formed the Chung Hua Keming Jun, Loo joined. Later he became a Tung Meng Hui member.[48]

Tam Wai-gum 譚惠金 (Dates unknown)

Tam Wai-gum joined the Chung Hua Keming Jun and in 1910 became a member of the Tung Meng Hui.[49] He had a business in Hilo and later moved to California.[50] He was the person who signed the canceled check made to the order of Sun Yat-sen in 1904.

MEMBERS OF THE TUNG MENG HUI IN HAWAII, 1910–1912

Loo Sun 盧信 (?–1933)

Loo Sun was a journalist working for the Hong Kong *Chung Kwok Yi Bo*, which was the official newspaper of the Hsing Chung Hui in Hong Kong. In 1907, when the *Tan San Sun Bo* was reorganized to become the *Ming Sun Yat Bo*, Loo Sun was hired to be the editor and came to Honolulu. One year later, Loo Sun emphasized freedom of speech and changed the name of the newspaper to *Chee Yow Shin Bo* (Liberty News). Loo was editor till 1911, when he returned to China. When the Tung Meng Hui Hawaii chapter was founded in Honolulu, he was elected secretary at the first meeting.[51]

LEONG HOY 梁海 (Dates unknown)

Leong Hoy was the owner of a store selling textiles in Honolulu's Chinatown. In 1910, he attended the first meeting of the Tung Meng Hui in Honolulu and was elected chairman. He was very supportive of the *Chee Yow Shin Bo*. He was awarded a citation by Sun Yat-sen in 1912.[52]

HEE TONG 許棠 (Dates unknown)

Hee Tong was a worker at the Honolulu Iron Works. When Sun Yat-sen was in Honolulu, he was Sun's driver. He was one of the members who attended the first meeting of the Tung Meng Hui Hawaii chapter in Honolulu. His membership card, shown in chapter 1, carries the number 20, showing that he was one of the first to join.[53]

SUN FO 孫科 (1891–1973)

Sun Fo was Sun Yat-sen's son. He came to Hawaii in 1895 when he was four years old. In 1910, when he was studying at St. Louis High School in Honolulu, he worked after school at the newspaper *Chee Yow Shin Bo* as translator. He attended the first meeting of the Tung Meng Hui in Honolulu and was a member. He returned to China after the Republic of China was established and later became the director of the Legislative Yuan. After 1950, he went to live in California for a while. Later, he went to Taiwan and died there. He married Chun Shuk-ying, who was born and grew up in Honolulu. They had two sons and two daughters. One son, Sun Tse-ping, is now living in Taiwan; the other son, Tse-keong Sun, lives in California. One daughter, Pearl Sui-ying Sun Lin, lives in Campbell, California, and the other daughter, Rose Sui-hua Sun Tchang, lives in San Diego, California.[54]

CHING CHOW 程就 (1877–1953)

Ching Chow was born in China and came to Hawaii when he was fourteen years old. After working in the Hung Kee store for a few years, he bought the store. He was first a director and then president of Liberty Bank in Honolulu. He founded the store Wing Hong Yuen Company, located at 177 North King Street. As he was a close friend of Sun Yat-sen, when Sun visited Honolulu, Sun stayed in the room on the second floor of the store. Ching Chow attended the first meeting of the Tung Meng Hui Hawaii chapter in Honolulu and was an active member. Ching Chow's home was located at 1127C Banyan Street, near Palama Street, in Honolulu, and Sun stayed there a number of times. Now this house is a private residence. Ching Chow provided part of the educational expenses of Sun's son, Sun Fo, when the latter was studying at St. Louis High School. Sun brought koa-wood furniture from Kula as gifts to Ching Chow. After Sun left Honolulu, he wrote to Ching, but Ching unfortunately burned the letters after reading them.[55]

YOUNG KWONG-TAT 楊廣達 (1869–1933)

Young Kwong-tat was born in Buck Toy, Leong Doo, Chung Shan District, and came to Hawaii in 1883. In 1896, he started the Wing Chong Loong Company and in 1901, the Kwong Chong Loong Company. He was a member the Chung Hua Keming Jun and later the chairman of the Tung Meng Hui Hawaii secret chapter in Honolulu. His store, Kwong Chong Loong, was the center where Tung Meng Hui members in Hawaii held their meetings. After the Tung Meng Hui was reorganized into the Kuomintang, he continued to be the chairman of the Kuomintang Hawaii branch from 1913 to 1915 and in 1917. He was one of the most generous donors to the revolution and the Chinese newspaper *Chee Yow Shin Bo* as well as to the Wah Mun School. His son, Young Wah-duck, is now the principal of the school, which has been renamed the Chung Shan School. Young Kwong-tat returned to China in 1922 and was the mayor of Chung Shan for many years. In 1933, he died in his native village.[56]

CHANG WING 鄭永 (1868–?)

Chang Wing was born in Hao Tou, Kwangtung Province, and came to Hawaii in 1895. He first opened a tailor shop, then a merchandise store. In 1910, he joined the Tung Meng Hui, later the Kuomintang. He raised money for the National Fund and was awarded a silver medal of the third class by Sun Yat-sen in 1924.[57]

LOUI KWAN-JUN 雷官進 (1878–1942)

Loui Kwan-jun was born in Hawaii and studied at Punahou School. He was one of the partners of the Sing Chong Company and owned many other businesses. He was a member of Tung Meng Hui and was one of those who attended the first meeting. He was also a member and one of the trustees of the Tung Meng Hui secret chapter in Honolulu. Loui's son, Owen Loui, said he heard family members talk of Sun Yat-sen's staying in their home, which was then located on Cunha Street, near Kukui Street, in Honolulu.[58]

TAM KWAI 譚遠 (Dates unknown)

Tam Kwai was a manager of an automobile service station in Honolulu. He was not one of the wealthiest among those who supported the revolution, but he was very generous in donations to the revolution and to the newspaper *Chee Yow Shin Bo*. He was a member of the Tung Meng Hui secret chapter in Honolulu.⁵⁹

CHOCK LUN 卓麟 (Dates unknown)

Chock Lun was the editor of the book *Chinese of Hawaii*. He was born in the village of Goon Tong, Kung Sheong Doo, Chung Shan District, and came to Hawaii in 1909. He received his English education at Mills School and the Iolani School. He was a translating editor for the *Chee Yow Shin Bo* and interpreter and translator for the National Recovery Act headquarters in Honolulu. He served as a correspondent for the *Star-Bulletin,* covering stories of the local Chinese community. In 1928, with Dr. Min Hin Li and Dormant C. Chang, he organized the Overseas Penman Club, and in the following year, the first edition of *Chinese of Hawaii* was published. In 1910, he joined in the Tung Meng Hui, later the Chung Hua Keming Tang and the Kuomintang.⁶⁰

CHUN K. MOY 陳國梅 (1893–?)

Chun K. Moy was born in Honolulu in 1893. He was a carpenter and was active in the Carpenters' Union in Honolulu. He joined in the Tung Meng Hui, later the Chung Hua Keming Tang.⁶¹

HEE KWONG 許廣 (1879-?)

Hee Kwong was born in Honolulu. His parents were from Chung Shan District. After working twelve years as a Chinese interpreter at the Immigration Station in Honolulu, he left and became president and manager of the United Trust Company. In 1922, he and friends formed Liberty Bank, and he was the cashier. He was generous in donating to the revolution. He joined the Tung Meng Hui and was very supportive of the newspaper *Chee Yow Shin Bo*.⁶²

Hung Hoy 洪海 (1876–?)

Hung Hoy was born in Shekki, Chung Shan, Kwangtung Province. He came to Hawaii in 1898 and was a merchant in Honlulu. He acted as a temporary director of the Tai Hung Company, which was a Shanghai corporation of Honolulu Chinese capital. He was a member of the Tung Meng Hui.[63]

Lee Chow 李秋 (1876–?)

Lee Chow was born in Shekki, Kwangtung Province. He came to Hawaii in 1895. He was the proprietor of Quon Wo Dress Making shop and founded the Dressmakers' Guild in Honolulu, which has since been dissolved. He joined the Tung Meng Hui in 1910 and later became a member of the Kuomintang.[64]

Leong Kwong 梁羅光 (1866–?)

Leong Kwong was a native of Jar Boo Tan village. He came to Hawaii in 1880 and was in the dry-goods, restaurant, and bakery businesses. He also operated rice plantations. He was a member of the Tung Meng Hui.[65]

Lum Hong-chee 林康敘 (1883–1960)

Lum Hong-chee was born in Honolulu. His father came from Nam Dai Chung, Chung Shan District. Lum Hong-chee was assistant cashier of the Chinese American Bank, Ltd., Honolulu. He joined the Tung Meng Hui and later, the Kuomintang. He was an editor of the *Han Ming Bo,* the official newspaper of the Hoong Moon Fraternity. He was also president of the Chinese-English Debating Society.[66]

Lum Hop 林合 (1853–?)

Lum Hop was a native of Hang Chin, Chung Shan District. He was one of the founders as well as a shareholder of C. Q. Yee Hop & Company. He joined the Tung Meng Hui and later, the Kuomintang.[67]

Lum Kan 林近 (1877–1957)

Lum Kan was also known as L. Akana. He was a native of Leong Doo. He came to Hawaii in 1898 and was a lumber yard foreman at C. K. Ai's City Mill Company. Later, he became the manager of a grocery store and a butcher shop. He was once the president of the *Chee Yow Shin Bo*. He was a member of the Tung Meng Hui and later the Kuomintang.[68]

Tam Yee 譚餘 (1866–?)

Tam Yee was a native of Wong Ning Tong village of Chung Shan District. He lived in Hawaii for a little over forty years. He was a licensed pharmacist and a member of Benson, Smith & Company, Ltd., one of the largest drug stores in Honolulu. He joined the Tung Meng Hui and later the Kuomintang.[69]

Wong Hing-chow 黃慶洲 (1860-1928)

Wong Hing-chow was a native of Tai Dum village, Chung Shan District. He came to Honolulu in 1876 and was employed as a bookkeeper at Wing Chong Loong Company. In 1891, he resigned and founded the Yee Shun Kee Dry Goods Store. He was a member of the Tung Meng Hui.[70]

WONG BUT-TING (Wong Lum) 黃弼廷 (1879–1946)

Wong But-ting was a native of Lung Doo, Chung Shan District. He was the proprietor of the Yat Sing dry-goods store on King Street in Honolulu. He was one of the founders of the Chinese American Bank in Honolulu. He studied and admired Sun Yat-sen's Three Principles of the People and joined the Tung Meng Hui in 1910.[71]

YEE LONG WO 余琅和 (1872–?)

Yee Long Wo came to Hawaii in 1888. He was the owner of a laundry. He was a member of the Chung Hua Keming Jun and later the Tung Meng Hui. When Sun Yat-sen was detained by immigration authorities in San Francisco in 1910, Yee telegraphed Wong San-duck, the president of the Chee Kong Tong in San Francisco, to help Sun. He was once the vice-president of the Tung Meng Hui Hawaii chapter.[72]

YOUNG HOOK-ING 楊福榮 (1890–1965)

Young Hook-ing was a native of Sun Ming Tung village. He came to Hawaii in 1912. Before he came to Hawaii, he joined the Tung Meng Hui in Macao. He was a teacher in the Wah Mun School for three years. Later, he went to Hilo and was manager of Ah Mai Company. He was a member of the Kuomintang and also the secretary of the National Fund-Raising Bureau in Honolulu in 1912.[73]

YOUNG AHIN 楊然 (Young Zhu-kun 楊著昆) (1853–1931)

Young Ahin came from Buck Toy, Leong Doo, Chung Shan District. He came to Hawaii in 1873 and became a rice planter, managing large-acreage rice fields and rice mills. He was also successfully involved in finance and real estate. He generously contributed to the revolution without much public recognition. According to the biographical sketch published in *The Chinese of Hawaii* in 1929, he received citations from Sun Yat-sen. He often hosted Sun in his house on Auld Lane and on Makiki Street.

After 1911, when the Chinese in Hawaii formed the National Fund-Raising Bureau, Young Ahin was the treasurer of the Bureau.[74] In 1921, he donated enough money to buy four airplanes for the Chinese air force.[75] Young Ahin was a member of the Kuomintang.[76]

WONG KWON 王堃 (Dates unknown)
Wong Kwon was one of the shareholders of the Yat Sing Cheong Company. He attended the first meeting of the Tung Meng Hui and was generous in supporting the revolution.[77]

YOUNG SEN-YAT (Yang Xian-yi) 楊仙逸 (1891–1923)
Young Sen-yat, Young Ahin's son, was born in Honolulu. As a youth, he listened to Sun Yat-sen talk about the revolution and was impressed and decided to join. He was a member of the Tung Meng Hui in Honolulu.

He studied and graduated from Iolani School and, in 1909, the College of Hawaii. He studied mechanics and aviation in California and at the Curtis Aviation School in Buffalo, New York. After he received his pilot's license as Hawaii's first Island-born land and seaplane pilot, he went to China in 1918 and organized China's first air force. Sun Yat-sen called him, the "Father of China's air force." In 1921, he traveled to Japan, Mexico, and the United States to raise funds for the Chinese air force. He managed to buy twelve J-M planes and equipment. He also recruited some patriotic young overseas Chinese to return to China and work for the air force. In February 1923, he was assigned as the chief of aviation of the Kwangtung government and the chief executive of the airplane factory in Kwangtung. He manufactured the first Chinese airplane and named it *Rosamond,* which was the English name of Soong Ching Ling (Madame Sun Yat-sen). During the first flight of this plane, Madame Sun was one of the passengers.

In 1923, during the battle against the warlord Chen Jiong-ming, who started a rebellion against Sun Yat-sen, Young was killed at Mei Hu, Bo Luo, on September 20, 1923. Sun Yat-sen conferred on him posthumously the rank of general and also wrote a scroll: "To the family members of Yang Xian-yi; Aim High to Reach the Heaven; Sun Wen [signed]."[78]

Young Sen-yat's son, Young Tim-oy, visited China in 1982 and presented the original scroll to the Sun Yat-sen Memorial Hall in Canton. He also donated generously to the Sen-yat School in Shekki, Kwangtung, named after his father.[79]

Young Sen-yat's grandson, Leigh-wai Doo, is an attorney in Honolulu and was a member of the Honolulu City Council from 1983 to 1994. He is also the president and one of the founding directors of the Dr. Sun Yat-sen Hawaii Foundation.

FIGURE 3.38. Sun Yat-sen and Soong Ching Ling with the airplane *Rosamond*. Photo courtesy Leigh-wai Doo.

FIGURE 3.39. Scroll written and signed by Sun Yat-sen. Photo courtesy of Leigh-wai Doo.

Yuan Yim 袁永 (1880–1965)

Yuan Yim was a native of Siu Yun village Chung Shan District. He was the president of the Acme Auto Company, Ltd., of Honolulu. He served as the president of the *Chee Yow Shin Bo* and joined the Tung Meng Hui. He was active in fund-raising for the National Fund-Raising Bureau and was awarded a medal by Sun Yat-sen.[80]

THE TUNG MENG HUI MAUI CHAPTER

Dang Hu 鄧富 (1880–1947)

Dang Hu of Paia, Maui, was a native of Seong Chark village, Chung Shan District. He came to Hawaii in 1897. He was the proprietor and manager of the Luke Kee store in Paia, dealing in general merchandise. He first joined the Tung Meng Hui, later the Chung Hua Keming Tang and the Kuomintang. He received a medal for distinguished service from Sun Yat-sen.[81]

Dang Ming-san 鄧明山 (1891–?)

Dang Ming-san was born in Hoy Ping District of Kwangtung Province and came to Hawaii in 1908. He became a merchant in Kahului and was the proprietor of the Wailuku Poi Factory and grocery store. Shortly after his arrival in Maui, he joined the Tung Meng Hui. He held various positions in the Maui branch of the Kuomintang, the Chung Hua Keming Tang, and the Chinese Kuomintang. Most of the time, he served as treasurer or as a member of the supervisory committee. For his work in the party, he won a silver medal awarded by Sun Yat-sen in 1922.[82]

LAU PANG (L. Apana) 劉聘 (1865–?)

Lau Pang was born in Tung Goon District, Kwangtung Province, and came to Hawaii in 1884. He was the proprietor of the L. Apana dry goods and tailoring store in Kahului, Maui. He joined the Tung Meng Hui Maui chapter in 1910 and later the Kuomintang Maui branch. In 1921 and 1923, he was commissioned by Sun Yat-sen to be the chairman of the Kuomintang Maui branch and a trustee of the Central Fund-Raising Bureau.[83]

LEE TAI-SAU 李齊秀 (1885–?)

Lee Tai-sau was a native of Toyshan, Kwangtung Province. He was the proprietor and manager of the Lee Sau Tailor Shop in Maui. He joined the Hsing Chung Hui Maui chapter when he was very young. He joined the Tung Meng Hui and was active in propagating the ideas of the revolution and in fund-raising. Later, he became a member of the executive committee of the Kuomintang Maui branch.[84]

TAM AH-FOOK 譚貴福 (1872–?)

Tam Ah-fook was a native of Sam Chow village, Chungshan District. He came to Hawaii in 1906 and had been in business ever since. He was in the restaraunt business and proprietor of the T. Ah Fook Store, Kahului, Maui. He was a prominent figure in the Maui Chinese community and a member of the Tung Meng Hui in Maui. Later he was a member of the executive committee of the territorial Kuomintang.[85]

APPENDIX I

Extracts from Punahou School Archives

CATALOGUE

OF THE

𝕮𝖗𝖚𝖘𝖙𝖊𝖊𝖘, 𝕿𝖊𝖆𝖈𝖍𝖊𝖗𝖘 𝖆𝖓𝖉 𝕻𝖚𝖕𝖎𝖑𝖘

OF

OAHU COLLEGE.

COMPILED BY ORDER OF THE TRUSTEES.

JUNE, 1883.

HONOLULU:
PRINTED AT THE "HAWAIIAN GAZETTE" OFFICE.
1881.

Extracts from Punahou School Archives *(continued)*

NAMES OF PUPILS. 9

Walker, Annie S.
Walker, Agnes
Woodard, Kate
Way, Alice M.
Weber, Victoria M.—117
Waterhouse, Nellie
Waterhouse, Fred. J. P.
Young, Agnes
Young, Susie

STUDENTS, 1882-1883.

ACADEMIC COURSE—SENIOR.

Alexander, Arthur C.
Green, May T.
Hillebrand, Mary E.
Hillebrand, Helen L.—4

SENIOR MIDDLE.

Baldwin, Winnifred M.
Emmes, Eliza E.
McDougal, William P.—3

JUNIOR MIDDLE.

Austin, Marion C.
Babcock, John M.
Beka, David K.
Forbes, Maria R.
Lishman, Isabella
Lowrey, Nellie M.
McIntyre, Frank P.
Mossman, Aimee
Peterson, Addie B.
Rogers, Kate
Sorrenson, Annie M.
Walker, Margaret J.—12

JUNIOR.

Aea, Paul
Atherton, Charles H.
Alexander, Henry M.
Carter, J. O. Jr.
Dickson, Bessie J.
Fuller, Belle M.
Greeve, Jennie R.
Hookano, Jackson
Hipa, Nahora J.
Johnson, Enoch
Liwai, Joseph
Low, John S.
Love, Alice
Lyman, Lilian
Sorrenson, Helen K.
Tisdale, Louise L.
Way, Alice M.
Walker, Annie S.—18

PREPARATORY COURSE—SECOND YEAR.

Brown, Arthur M.
Benson, Maud
Carter, Alfred W.
Carter, Cara
Cooke, Joseph P.
Campbell, Ida R.

10 NAMES OF PUPILS.

Coney, Ellen
Cleghorn, Annie P.
Clark, Sarah
Clark, Cornelia
Dillingham, May
Forbes, William J.
Ford, Seth P.
Gilliland, R. L.
Greig, William H.
Hall, Horace V.
Horner, Robert
Horner, Annie
Hurd, Catherine J.
Hitchcock, Mary R.
Ii, Airene H.
Koki, David
Koki, Moses
Kinney, Annie
Lewers, Frederick
Lawlor, William
McGuire, Joseph
Mossman, Edward E.
Nott, Catherine
Renton, Emma M.
Renton, Alice M.
Thrum, George E.
Toler, James H.
Waterhouse, S. P.
Waterhouse, Nellie
Wall, Walter
Weber, Victoria M.
Woodard, Kate—38

FIRST YEAR.

Allen, George C.
Bindt, Franz B.
Bindt, Edward J.
Benfield, L.
Brown, Minnie H.
Butler, Lily
Cummings, Homer
Coney, Lizzie
Dickson, Laurita
Forbes, Hattie
Halstead, Robert E.
Piikoi, Edward
Piikoi, Jonah
Pratt, Lewellyn
Penniman, Bessie A.
Rogers, Edmund H.
Reed, Wesley
Robinson, William S.
Rickard, Emma
Rickard, Louise
Savidge, William
Thrum, William F.
Hitchcock, Hattie C.
Hessinger, Juanita
Jones, Ada
Lee, Chung
Nott, Annie W.
Piikoi, David K.
Tai, Chu
Tong, Hong
Walker, John
Walker, Agnes
Weik, Hermann—33

The name "Tai Chu" is under "First Year," second column.

APPENDIX II

Punahou Alumni Directory Information Card

```
          1923              INFORMATION CARD — PUNAHOU ALUMNI DIRECTORY

NAME IN FULL (Last name first)    TAI, CHOCK ;  also known as SEN, DR. SUN YAT

DATE (Year) OF DIPLOMA, if any, from Oahu College or Punahou Academy

IF NON-GRADUATE, Year your class graduated from Oahu College—Ex.

IN ELEMENTARY SCHOOL from              to              ; from              to
          or
IN PREPARATORY SCHOOL from             to              ; from              to

IN JUNIOR ACADEMY from                 to              ; from              to

IN ACADEMY OR OAHU COLLEGE from  1882  to    1883      ; from              to

COLLEGE DEGREES (Name college and year degree conferred)

NAME IN FULL OF HUSBAND OR WIFE

PRESENT OCCUPATION

PERMANENT ADDRESS

PRESENT MAILING ADDRESS
```

APPENDIX III

Extract from Punahou School Ledger, 1881–1885

APPENDIX IV

Members Who Attended the First Meeting of the Hsing Chung Hui 興中會, Honolulu, November 24, 1894

Ai, C. K. 鍾工宇
Chang Chau 鄭照
Chang Kim 鄭金
Ching Wai-nam 程蔚南
Chock Hai 卓海
Chow Choy 曹彩
Chun Nam 陳南
Chung Mook-heen 鍾木賢
Dang Ying-nam[1] 鄧蔭南
Ha Park-chee 夏百子
Hee Jack-son 許直臣
Ho Fon 何寬

How Ai-chin 侯艾泉
Lau Cheong 劉祥
Lau Chock 劉卓
Lau Sau 劉壽
Lee Chong 李昌
Lee Kai 李杞
Lee Look 李祿
Lee To-ma 李多馬
Lum Kam-chin 林鑑泉
Soong Kee-yun 宋居仁
Wong Leong 黃亮
Wong Wah-fei 黃華恢

Officers Elected

Chairman: Lau Cheong 劉祥
Vice-chairman: Ho Fon 何寬

Treasurer: Wong Wah-fei 黃華恢

Source: Feng Tzu-yu, *Unofficial History of the Revolution* (Taipei: Commercial Press, 1965), 4:3.

APPENDIX V

Hsing Chung Hui Members and Ledger of Dates and Payments of Membership Fees

The original ledger was written in a notebook that was in Ho Fon's keeping for thirty years. It was first reproduced in the 1929 edition of *The Chinese in Hawaii—History*, published by the Overseas Penman Club, Honolulu (pages 16–17). The following is a translation.

NAMES AND DATES OF PAYMENTS

November 24, 1894
Ho Fon 何寬, Lee Chong 李昌

November 28, 1894
Wei Chock-sing 衛積盛

November 29, 1894
Lee Kwong-fai 李光輝, Wong Ming Fong 黃綿鳳, Ho Han 何旱, Soong Kee-yun 宋居仁

December 6, 1894
Lau Chock 劉卓, Lum Kam-chin 林鑑泉, Lee To-ma 李多馬, Ching Hung-sum 程恒心, Zane Sing 曾勝, Chung Meng-him 陳孟謙

December 7, 1894
Yap Kwai-fong 葉桂芳

December 10, 1894
Wong Leong 黃亮

December 11, 1894
C. K. Ai 鍾工宇

December 13, 1894
Ching Wai-nam 程蔚南

December 20, 1894
Wan Yuk-chin 尹煜傳, Hee Jack-son 許直臣, Ha Park-chee 夏百子, Wong Hung-pui 黃慶培

January 3, 1895
Woo Mui 胡眛, Lee Yeh 李月, Luke Mun-wah 陸望華, Young Nap 楊納, Moo Yan-fook 巫恩福

January 3, 1895
Chang Fat 鄭發, Goo Yee 古義

January 17, 1895
Leong Bun 梁賓

January 21, 1895
Chang Chung-chew 鄭仲昭, Auyong Fong 歐陽晃, Xu Chun 許振, Wong Yee 黃二, Tam Butt 譚弼, Young Tin-hee 容天煦, Young Duck-cho 楊德初, Fong Chin 鄺全, Tam Ray 譚瑞, Young Ji-cho 容吉兆, Sun Mei 孫眉, Luke Tan-sung 陸檀生, Lau Tang 劉登, Wong Chock-shan 黃卓山. Dang Soong-sing 鄧松盛 recommended fifteen members: Chun Tin-yong 陳天養, Hung Ming 馮明, Dang Hin-duck 鄧顯德, Dang Soong-sing 鄧松盛, Dang Hop 鄧合, Ng Yee-yap 伍于洽, Ng Ah-loy 伍亞來, Ng Jun-duck 吳俊德, Ng Yuen-duck 吳元德, Wong Boo 黃保, Lau Chung 劉宗, Chang Chi-kam 鄭子見, Lum Pui 林培, Dang Kui-duck 鄧貴德, Dang Wah-choi 鄧華彩.

February 28, 1895
Young Pak-kwai 楊伯貴, Lau Lo-fat 劉羅發

April 17, 1895
Lai Young 賴養, Tsou Duck-ming 鄒德明, Hung Wing-ming 馮永明, Lee Yang-kwai 李潤貴, Wong Mok 黃木, Chong Ting 張丁, Lee Lok 李六, Chung Mook-heen 鍾木賢, Lau Cheong 劉祥, Chong Fook-yee 張福如, Chock Hoy[1] 卓海, Lee Chau 李照, Hee Jun 許進, Chang Kim 鄭金, Hee Dai-yau 許帝有.

April 20, 1895
Ching Nam 陳南

April 22, 1895
Chun Ng-wo 陳五和, Lai Hin-cheong 黎顯祥, Wong Sun 黃純, Lee Chew 李超, Ng Hung 吳桓, Chock Hoy 卓海, Chun Kun-kwon 陳檻君, Tai Dwai 戴貴, Lee Lum 李林, Kan Wing-chew 簡永照, Sui Yee-sing 蕭義勝

May 2, 1895
Ching Chu-on 程祖安, Lau Sum 劉森

May 8, 1895
Leong Chuck-poo 梁澤袍, Lum Fai 林輝, Chun Dai-tong 陳帝棠, Ching Dao 程道, Lock Lai 駱禮, Chow Choy 曹彩, Lee Oi-wan 李靄雲, Lum Duck-kau 林德珠, Ho Yee 何義, Wong How 黃後, Chung Bing-kai 陳炳階, Ching Yee-tin 程雨亭

September 2, 1895
Ng Wan-sung 伍雲生, Oo Sau 鄔秀, Hu Ting 胡廷, Chong Ting-kwai 張丁貴, Ng Jun 伍珍, Lee Lun 李綸, Wong Chau 黃秋, Zane Wai-kao 曾維高, Yap Kim 葉金, Lee Kai 李杞, How Yee-chin 侯義全

The members listed above each paid membership fees of $5.00. Soong Kee-yun paid $3.00.

Total income from membership fees: $288.00

INCOME

Dang Soong-sing 鄧松盛 bought shares $300.00
Hawaiians bought shares $200.00
Goong Tong 古同 bought shares $100.00
Chang Chung 鄭仲 bought shares $100.00
Young Gut-chew 容吉兆 bought shares $100.00
Sun Mei 孫眉 bought shares $200.00
Lee To-ma 李多馬 bought shares $100.00
Total from shares $1,100.00
grand total: $1,388.00

PAYMENTS

To Sun Yat-sen 孫逸仙 $1,004.00
To Sun Yat-sen 孫逸仙 $100.00 (his own money)
Paid telegram to Shanghai $20.80
total payments: $1,160.00
balance: $227.20

February 26, 1895, paid Soong Kee-yun 宋居仁 $25.00 for travel expenses to China.

APPENDIX VI

Members of the Chung Hua Keming Jun 中華革命軍 (Chinese Revolutionary Army), Formed in Hilo, 1903

Chang Chung 鄭仲
Chang Hou 鄭豪
Chang Jock 鄭爵
Chang Pun 鄭盆
Chang Yee 鄭義
Chang Yuk 鄭旭
Goo Ho 古賀
Lee Wah-gum 李華根
Lum Han-nam 林翰南
Lum Butt-nam 林弼南
Mao Man-ming 毛文明
Tang Cheong 唐長
Wong Chau 黃灶
Wong Chi 黃賜
Wong Gum 黃根
Young Chee 楊吉
Young Yin 楊衍

Source: Su Teh-yung, "The Founding Father's Revolutionary Activities in Hawaii," in *The Historical Material of Overseas Chinese in the Revolution of the Founding of the Republic* (Taipei: Zheng Chung Book Co., 1977), 77.

APPENDIX VII

Members Who Joined the Teng Meng Hui in 1910

MEMBERS WHO JOINED THE FIRST TUNG MENG HUI MEETING, MARCH 1910

Ching Chow 程就
Fong Leong 鄺良
Goo Pak-chin 古柏荃
Hee Jack-son 許直臣
Hee Tong 許棠
Leong Hoy 梁海
Loo Koon 盧冠
Loo Sun 盧信
Loui Kwan-jun 雷官進
Lum Kong 林光
Lum Gau 林覺
Sun Fo 孫科
Tam Kwai 譚逵
Wen Phong-fei 溫雄飛
Wong Kwon 王堃
Zane Chong-fook 曾長福

Officers Elected

Chairman: Leong Hoy 梁海
Secretary: Loo Sun 盧信
Treasurer: Zane Chong-fook 曾長福

MEMBERS WHO JOINED THE SECRET CHAPTER OF THE TUNG MENG HUI, HONOLULU, APRIL 1910

C. K. Ai 鍾工宇
Lee Lap 李烈
Loo Sun 盧信
Loui Kwan-jun 雷官進
Tam Leong 譚亮
Tam Kwai 譚逵
Wong Leong 黃亮
Young Kwong-tat 楊廣達

Officers Elected

Chairman: Young Kwong-tat 楊廣達
Secretary: Loo Sun 盧信
Treasurer: Lee Lap 李烈
Trustees: Tam Kwai 譚逵,
Loui Kwan-jun 雷官進,
C. K. Ai 鍾工宇, Wong Leong 黃亮

MEMBERS WHO JOINED THE TUNG MENG HUI, MAUI, 1910

Dang Ming-san 鄧明山
Lau Pang 劉聘
Luke Jun 陸進
Tam Jun 譚進
Tam Kui-fook 譚貴福

Source: Feng Tzu-yu, *Unofficial History of the Revolution* (Taipei: Commercial Press, 1965), 4:177.

APPENDIX VIII

Members of the Tung Meng Hui, Hilo, 1910

In Hilo, 385 members joined the Tung Meng Hui in 1910. They were organized like an army. There were two companies. In each company, there were four platoons, and in each platoon, there were twelve squads. The following are the names of the leaders.

FIRST COMPANY

Leader

Lai Hip 黎協　(Lai Kwok-ming 黎國民)

Platoon Leaders

Chang Sung-goong 鄭成功　　Yang Sui 楊水
Wong Chow 黃灶　　　　　　Lee Wah-geng 李華根

Squad Leaders

Tong Cheong 唐長　　　　　Young Yun-yuen 楊潤元
Chun Doong 陳東　　　　　Young Yik 楊益
Chiu Gao-lun 趙旭倫　　　　Chun Tu-gun 陳土根
Chun Sung 陳成　　　　　　Chang Fat 鄭發
Leong Gao 梁九　　　　　　Lee Sung-goong 李成功
Chow Sam-fook 周三福　　　Chock Kwok-jun 卓國禎

SECOND COMPANY

Leader

Loo Sian 盧先

Platoon Leaders

Chow Kin 周敬　　　　　　Tam Wai-gum 譚惠金
Chang Si-doo 鄭世鐸　　　　Wang Kwai-fun 黃桂芬

Squad Leaders

Au Ho 歐賀　　　　　　　　Chang Butt 鄭弼
Chiu Jun 趙珍　　　　　　　Lum Doong-sau 林東秀
Woo Gum-chiu 胡錦釗　　　Chang Sun 鄭信
Chun Chiu 陳全　　　　　　Chang Duck 鄭德
Gung Mai-how 龔買好　　　Lee Dung-hung 李定宏
Liu Hung 廖慶

Source: *The Chinese of Hawaii—History* (Honolulu: Overseas Penman Club, 1929), 31.

APPENDIX IX

News Item from the Chinese *People's Daily* (Overseas Edition), August 26. 1985

人民日報（海外版）　1985年8月26日

林文光贈獻孫中山書信手跡

據新華社北京八月二十五日電　美籍華人林文光先生最近將他珍藏多年的孫中山先生的一封親筆信、兩封簽名信等珍貴歷史文物贈獻給了孫中山研究學會。

林文光先生的父親林智早年居住在美國夏威夷，曾追隨孫中山先生從事反對滿清政府的革命活動。林智先生生前一直珍藏着這些珍貴的歷史文物，並叮囑自己的子女，一定要把這些文物送回祖國。

宋慶齡基金會副主席吳全衡和孫中山研究學會副會長劉大年在贈獻儀式上讚揚了林智和林文光先生的愛國熱情。劉大年說，這些文物對孫中山的研究工作有較高的價值。

TRANSLATION

Mung Kong Lum Donated Letter Written by Sun Yat-sen

Xin-hua News Agency, August 15, Beijing: Mr. Lum Mung-kong, an American Chinese, donated to the Sun Yat-sen Society a letter written and signed by Mr. Sun Yat-sen's, two letters signed by Mr. Sun and other historical documents that he kept carefully for a long time.

Mr. Lum Chee, Lum Mung-kong's father, immigrated to Hawaii a long time ago. He was a follower of Mr. Sun Yat-sen and participated in revolutionary activities against the Manchu regime. Mr. Lum Chee kept all these documents and told his son to donate these precious documents to the motherland where they belong.

APPENDIX X

Two Letters of Condolence Sun Yat-sen Sent to Hilo after Lai Hip's Death

為黎協遇害致希爐同志函　民國四年（一九一五年）

逕啓者：接檀香山籌餉局長吳君鐵城十一月二十六日來函，內稱貴分局長兼籌餉局長黎君協，於上月十九日為兇人所害，驚聞之下，痛悼殊深。查黎君奔走國事，不避艱瘁，兩年以來，黨務倚重甚力；現值討賊在卽，遽遭慘變，致令共志未終，飲恨地下，同志悲惋，曷可勝言。茲望諸君從速催饬法庭，將兇犯嚴訊治罪；並代向黎君家屬，申意吊唁，溫辭撫慰，以安黎君在天之靈。至分部餉局，雙方進行，刻不容緩，卽望名集同志，另舉相當者接續辦理，以重黨務，而專責成。實為至盼。此啓希爐分部、希爐籌餉局同志諸公均鑒。並頌時祉。孫文。十二月十四日。

覆黃根等追悼黎協並囑籌款討賊函　民國五年（一九一六年）

黃根、劉家兩先生大鑒：復函已悉。黎君慘遭奸人毒手，弟驚聞之下，曷勝悼惜之至。貴分部開會追悼，並以遠隔萬里，未能躬與盛會，尤為憾事。所望黎君雖死，公等檔志有人，以覺黎君未竟之志，則黎君雖死之日，猶生之年，顧公等努力前途。貴處信箱，弟當另行存記，他日有函，自必按址寄上，請勿系念。貴處前後寓餉，已盡由美支節籌茨，公等熱心捐輸，同人無任紉感。目下內地革命，風雲日急，需款浩繁，仍冀公等朝夕籌濟，則將來驅除國賊，遂我自由，皆諸公之力也。匆此，並叩籌安。孫文。一月二十五日。

Source: Historical Commission of the Central Committee of the Chinese Kuomintang, ed., *Complete Works of the Founding Father* (Taipei: Central Supply Agency of Historical and Cultural Material, 1950).

TRANSLATION

First Letter of Condolence to the Family and the Chinese Revolutionary Party Hilo Branch, December 14, 1915

I received a letter from Mr. Wu Tie-cheng, the chief of the Fund-Raising Bureau of Hawaii, who informed me that Mr. Lai Hip, the chief of the Chinese Revolutionary Party Branch of Hilo and also the chief of the Fund-Raising Bureau of Hilo, was assassinated by a murderer. On hearing this news, I am so sorry and feel the pain and loss deeply. Mr. Lai worked hard for our country, and he never complained about the hardship and difficulties he had to go through. We relied heavily on him to work for our party. Now we are just going to launch a campaign against the enemy [that is, Yuan Shih-kai, who betrayed the Republic in trying to restore monarchy], and at this crucial time, Mr. Lai met his tragic death. His wishes have not been realized and he certainly would regret that. All the comrades feel sad and sorry. Hope you people would urge the court to proceed with the trial and punish the assailant.

Please extend my deep condolences to the family members of Mr. Lai Hip and also my many kind words I want to say to the family members. Wish Mr. Lai Hip peace in heaven.

As to the work of the party branch, trust you comrades would find someone to continue on with the job. This letter was addressed to the party branch of Hilo and the Fund-Raising Bureau of Hilo.

Sun Wen [signed], December 14.

Second Letter Addressed to Wong Gum and Lau On, January 15, 1916

To Mr. Wong Gum and Mr. Lau On: Your letter is duly received. Mr. Lai Hip was assassinated by the assailant. When I heard the news I was shocked and am terribly sorry and sad. My deep regrets for not being able to attend the memorial services and the funeral as I am thousands of miles away from Hawaii. Hope you could continue on with the job that Mr. Lai Hip was dedicated to with so much enthusiasm. Lai Hip would be happy to know that although he died, you people are continuing on to do the work that he wanted to do but could not finish.

The funds you sent over were duly received. Thank you for your generous contributions. The revolution against Yuan is going on well in China. One day, Yuan will be removed and China will regain freedom. This will all be possible because of your efforts and contributions.

Regards, Sun Wen [signed]

APPENDIX XI

News Item in the *Pacific Commercial Advertiser*, October 7, 1903. "Noted Reformer Sun Arrives Here Quietly"

NOTED REFORMER SUN ARRIVES HERE QUIETLY

Man Who Would Like to Overthrow the Dynasty of the Empress Dowager and Her Mandarins.

Dr. Sun Yat Sen, the famous Chinese revolutionist and reformer, the man who would create a Chinese republic upon the old empire, and whose name is known throughout the world, arrived from Yokohama on Monday as a passenger in the Siberia. Dr. Sun came to Honolulu quietly, as he generally does, and is at present the guest of friends here. He is a man yet young, who was educated at Iolani College, Honolulu, under Bishop Willis. His brother S. Ahuni, is the well-known Maui resident.

Dr. Sun came direct from Yokohama, where he has been, keeping in touch with the revolutionists in China. His plans regarding his stay in this city are indefinite although he may remain here for about three months, spending a portion of the time on Maui with his brother.

It has been the aim of Dr. Sun to overthrow the dynasty of the Empress Dowager and her mandarins. He is strongly of the opinion that radical reform in China can come only through the sweeping away of the Manchu dynasty and the adoption of foreign methods of administration.

In September 1900, Dr. Sun headed the great young China movement when an attempt was made to have the provinces in lower China rise up against the Imperial Government and overthrow it. It was an audacious move, for Dr. Sun, as a general, commanded only 600 men near Hongkong in an empire containing nearly 400,000,000 people. He intended to make an assault on the town of Wai Chow, calculating on the Imperial troops being withdrawn to put down a Bow Wong uprising elsewhere. He hoped to subjugate Foo Kin province and operate therefrom. That was to have been the beginning of the Chinese Republic. Some 4000 Imperial troops were sent against Dr. Sun. Then came an uprising, and for a while Dr. Sun's forces were victorious. But the failure of the Bow Wongs to operate elsewhere, defeated Dr. Sun's cherished plans. Finally, one of his leaders was captured and executed.

It has been his contention that the large sums of money raised have been of no avail in China, seemingly not used in the way that would bring results.

Dr. Sun may shortly address meetings of the Chinese on his favorite subject.

APPENDIX XII

News Item in the
Pacific Commercial Advertiser, December 14, 1903.
"Dr. Sun Advocates a Revolt in China"

DR. SUN ADVOCATES A REVOLT IN CHINA
Overthrow of the Manchu Dynasty Urged by the Famous Revolutionist---Emperor "Sick Man of the Far East."

Dr. Sun Yat Sen bids fair to become one of the world's noted men if all the plans he is presenting to the Chinese people of Hawaii and the Chinese Empire, are consummated.

The famous revolutionist spoke yesterday afternoon in the Chinese theater on Hotel street to a mass meeting of Chinese to whom he unfolded his views of the political situation in the Chinese Empire. Throughout his address he fearlessly stated that revolution in the Empire was the one event which would take China out of its present deplorable position with reference to the world powers and place it on a footing which would cause the nations to respect it. The overthrow of the Manchu dynasty, he said, should be undertaken by revolution, and this, in his opinion was to be a certainty. He strongly advocated that the Chinese of Hawaii back the revolutionary party in the attempt to overthrow the Empire and establish a Republic on its ruins.

Dr. Sun said that it was his great present dynasty is foreign to the Chinese people that so many centuries have elapsed since the Manchus became the rulers of the Empire that the Chinese have forgotten that the present dynasty is foreign to the Chinese people, as foreign as the Russians or the Japanese and that as soon as the Chinese people awake to this fact they will rise in a mighty, crushing revolution, and forever rid themselves of their oppressors.

Dr. Sun received with great enthusiasm and his speech was frequently punctuated with applause. The theater was packed from pit to gallery and even the stage was crowded. Dr. Sun appeared in cool linen, his dress and short-cropped hair giving him the appearance of a Filipino rather than a Chinese. As a speaker he showed unmistakable evidences of being an orator of considerable power. He has a prepossessing appearance, his gestures are impressive and he seemed to sway his audience at will. There was nothing of the fanatic or even the enthusiast in his appearance or manner. He appeared more a methodical, painstaking thinker, cool and collected, and born to be a leader, as he has already proven himself to be in the secret council of the revolutionists, or at the head of a determined band of Chinese revolutionists engaged in battle with the forces of the Chinese Emperor.

Dr. Sun, after a formal introduction, spoke directly to his subject, which was on the principles of revolution and what they meant to the Chinese people. His theme, he said, dealt entirely with the overthrow of the present dynasty, the government of the Manchus. Before the first dynasty the government was a sort of Republic, when the Emperor was selected by the people, a wise man in whom the people could repose their trust.

"The question is whether we ought to revolt against the present Manchu dynasty," he said.

"We ought to do so, we must do so!" exclaimed Dr. Sun vehemently, bringing his fist down upon a table at his side.

"Why? Because the present reigning house is that of a fallen conqueror, and second because it is not a house of our own Chinese race. According to the growing feeling and sentiment of patriotism the Emperor should be turned out whether he is a good or a bad ruler."

Dr. Sun sketched the misgovernment of the Manchu dynasty. Great slaughter of the Chinese people took place when the Manchus came into power. The Chinese submitted and ever since then the Manchu dynasty has devised skillful methods to prevent the Chinese people from rising in revolt. The Chinese have ethically submitted to every form of suffering until they are now a crushed race. The speaker said the Chinese people have little protection from foreign nations, as the Chinese government seems to care little for them. For this reason the Chinese people were not respected, and not on an equal footing with people of other nations. Under such conditions, even though the Emperor were one of their own race, they should rise and throw him out.

"The dynasty is decaying," continued the revolutionist. "If we, the Chinese people who should be governing our affairs, do not rise and turn out this Sick Man of the Far East, other powers will yet do so and then divide up the Empire. This is one of the most powerful reasons why we should rise and uproot the dynasty and restore the country again to its ancient people.

"The prosperity of China is now certain to assist in spreading the seeds of revolt over the vast Empire. We know the Manchus have become impotent. Their extreme weakness was apparent during the Boxer trouble. Then not more than 20,000 troops of the Allied Army marched upon Peking and captured the capital of the Empire. This is the midst of a nation of 400,000,000 of people. Think of it! Only 20,000 soldiers in that vast Empire and the Manchu government standing weakly by while it was done!

"If such an army of foreign soldiers could capture the capital, what would happen if the Chinese people rose in their might. They could take the capital much easier than did the Allies.

"There is no great difficulty before us in accomplishing this same result. The real difficulty lies in the fact that the people have not awakened to the fact that the Manchus are foreigners, as much so as the Russians or any other power. Centuries of suffering under the Manchu yoke have rendered the Chinese people callous to the knowledge of who their present rulers really are. But once the people are awakened and realize their own strength, we can easily devise an invulnerable plan to overthrow the Manchu dynasty and build upon its ruins a good government—the Republic of China."

NOTES

CHAPTER I

1. *A Chronological Biography of the Founding Father*, 3rd ed. (Taipei: Party History Committee of the Chinese Kuomintang, 1985), 1:24, 32, 38, 39, 68, 72, 85, 88, 189, 197, 340, 347. We have adopted the local Hawaiian Chinese way of spelling Chinese proper names. In referring to Sun Yat-sen's age, we have counted his age as one year old in 1867.
2. *At the Call We Gather: Iolani School* (Honolulu: Iolani School, 1997), 28.
3. Paul Linebarger, *Sun Yat Sen and the Chinese Republic* (New York: AMS Press, 1969), 125-126.
4. *Sun Yat-sen's Dream*, video made by the television station of Jiangsu Province, China, 1995; quotation from Jing Chong-ji, deputy director of the Chinese Documents Research Institute, Beijing.
5. Sun Yat-sen, "Hand-written Auto-Biography" (1896), written in London at the request of Herbert Allen Giles and published in *Manuscripts of the Founding Father* (Taipei: Historical Commission of the Central Committee of the Kuomintang, 1961), 1:5–6.
6. Albert Pierce Taylor, "Sun Yat Sen in Honolulu," *Paradise of the Pacific*, 41, no. 8 (August 1928):10.
7. Linebarger, *Sun Yat Sen and the Chinese Republic*, 116-117.
8. *Chronological Biography of the Founding Father*, 1:34.
9. Hsiang Ting-yung, *Founding Father's Seven Visits to the United States and Hawaii* (Taipei: Time Newspaper and Culture Publishing Company, 1982), 27.
10. Sun Yat-sen, "Auto-Biography," a narration of the ten uprisings before the founding of the Republic of China, in *San Min Zhuyi* (Taipei: Committee of the Million Copies of San Min Zhuyi, 1988), 2.
11. Feng Tzu-yu, *Unofficial History of the Revolution* (Taipei: Taiwan Commercial Press, 1965), 4:4.
12. Irma Tam Soong and Wei-tung Lin, *Five Hsing Chung Hui Men of Valor* (Taipei: Federation of Overseas Chinese Association Publishing House, 1989) 8.
13. Yansheng Ma Lum, interview with Chun Chee-kwon, August 1995.
14. Sun, "Auto-Biography," 3.

15. *Dictionary of the Hsin Hai Revolution* (Wuhan: Wuhan Publishing House, 1991), 158.
16. Su Teh-yung, "The Founding Father's Revolutionary Activities in Hawaii," in *Historical Material of Overseas Chinese in the Founding of the Republic* (Taipei: Zheng Chung Book Co., 1977), 71.
17. C. K. Ai, *My Seventy Nine Years in Hawaii* (Hong Kong: Cosmorama Pictorial Publisher, 1960), 315.
18. Feng, *Unofficial History*, 4:4.
19. Soong and Lin, *Five Hsing Chung Hui Men of Valor*, 151.
20. *The Revolutionary History of the Founding of the Republic of China* (Taipei: Da Tung Institute, 1929), 1:19.
21. Su, "The Founding Father's Revolutionary Activities," 71.
22. Yansheng Ma Lum, interview with William Tavares, April 1998.
23. Feng, *Unofficial History*, 1:10.
24. Peter Baldwin, president, Haleakala Ranch Company, Maui, letter to Yansheng Ma Lum, May 5, 1998.
25. Diane Mei Lin Mark, *The Chinese in Kula: Recollections of a Farming Community in Old Hawaii* (Honolulu: Hawaii Chinese History Center, Honolulu, 1975), 3.
26. Linebarger, *Sun Yat Sen and the Chinese Republic*, 101-102.
27. *The Revised Sun Chung-shan Chronology* (Guangzhou: Guangzhou Publishing House, 1998), 1:44.
28. Sun, "Auto-Biography," 2.
29. Yansheng Ma Lum, interview with Pang Hong-kwun, May 1998.
30. Yansheng Ma Lum, interview with Loo Ngan-sum, May 1998.
31. Yansheng Ma Lum, interview with William Tavares, April 1998.
32. Su, "The Founding Father's Revolutionary Activities," 71.
33. Sun, "Auto-Biography," 7.
34. *The Chinese of Hawaii-History* (Honolulu: Overseas Penman Club, 1929), 34–35.
35. Tin-Yuke Char and Wai Jane Char, *Chinese Historic Sites and Pioneer Families of the Island of Hawaii* (Honolulu: Hawaii Chinese History Center, 1983), 40.
36. Hsiang, *Founding Father's Seven Visits*, 83.
37. May Day Lo, "Hawaiians Knew Their Poi, Recalls 'Taro King' of Days of Monarchy," *Honolulu Star-Bulletin*, July 30, 1936.
38. Su, "Founding Father's Revolutionary Activities in Hawaii," 78–79.
39. Su, "Founding Father's Revolutionary Activities in Hawaii," 71–72.
40. *The Chinese of Hawaii-Newspaper* (1929), 63–64.
41. Feng, *Unofficial History*, 1:197; Hsiang, *Founding Father's Seven Visits*, 96–97.
42. Sun, "Auto-Biography," 22.
43. Feng, *Unofficial History*, 4:176–177.
44. Yansheng Ma Lum, interview with Owen Loui, December 1997.
45. Yansheng Ma Lum, interview with Ching Ping-quon, December 1997.
46. Taylor, "Sun Yat Sen in Honolulu," 8–11.
47. Yansheng Ma Lum, interview with Frank Eng, April 1998.
48. *The Chinese of Hawaii-History* (1929), 31.
49. Yansheng Ma Lum, interview with Elizabeth Lai Hip Lum, November 1998.

50. Feng, *Unofficial History,* 4:177.
51. Wen Phong-fei, "Recalling My Work With the Tung Meng Hui and Zi You Xin Bao in Hawaii Before 1911," in *The Hua Qiao and the Hsin Hai Revolution* (Beijing: Chinese Academy of Social Sciences, 1981), 234.
52. Wen, "Recalling My Work," 234–235.
53. Sun Yat-sen, *Complete Works* (Beijing: History Study Institute and others, Guangdong Provincial Academy of Science, 1981), 1:453.
54. Su, "Founding Father's Revolutionary Activities in Hawaii," 96.
55. Su, "Founding Father's Revolutionary Activities in Hawaii," 85.
56. Henry Bond Restarick, *Sun Yat Sen, Liberator of China* (New Haven: Yale University Press, 1931), 113–114.
57. *Chronological Biography,* 1:38.
58. Sun, *Complete Works,* 1:463.
59. Harold Z. Schiffrin, *Sun Yat-sen and the Origins of the Chinese Revolution* (Berkeley: University of California Press, 1968), 148.
60. Restarick, *Sun Yat Sen,* 46.
61. Neil L. Thomsen, "No Such Sun Yat-sen: An Archival Success Story," *Chinese America: History and Perspectives 1997* (San Francisco: Chinese Historical Society of America, 1997), 20–22.

CHAPTER II

1. Jiang Yung-jing, "Study of the Funding of the Ten Uprisings Before the Hsin Hai Revolution," in *Historical Material of Overseas Chinese in the Founding of the Republic* (Taipei: Zheng Chung Book Store, 1977), 40–41.
2. Chock Lun, "Chinese Organizations in Hawaii," in *The Chinese of Hawaii* (1936), 29.
3. Feng, *Unofficial History,* 4:4.
4. Sun, *Complete Works,* 1:421.
5. Soong and Lin, *Five Hsing Chung Hui Men of Valor,* 61.
6. Jiang, "Study of the Funding," 45.
7. Jiang, "Study of the Funding," 46.
8. Feng, *Unofficial History,* 4:223.
9. Hsiang, *Founding Father's Seven Visits,* 94.
10. Wen, "Recalling My Work," 245.
11. Hsiang, *Founding Father's Seven Visits,* 278.
12. Yansheng Ma Lum, interview with Young Wah-duck, April 1995.
13. Feng, *Unofficial History,* 1:235.
14. Sun, *Complete Works,* 1:463–464.
15. Sun, *Complete Works,* 1:469.
16. Sun, *Complete Works,* 1:486–487.
17. Su, "Founding Father's Revolutionary Activities in Hawaii," 86.
18. Feng, *Unofficial History,* 4:177.
19. Clarence E. Glick, *Sojourners and Settlers: Chinese Immigrants in Hawaii* (Honolulu: University Press of Hawaii, 1980), 127.

20. *Hilo Tribune*, November 23, 1915, November 30, 1915.
21. Hsiang, *Founding Father's Seven Visits*, 229–230.
22. Hsiang, *Founding Father's Seven Visits*, 251.
23. *The Chinese of Hawaii-History* (1929), 24.
24. Feng, *Unofficial History*, 4:175.
25. Wen, "Recalling My Work," 250; Wen Phong-fei, "Recalling My Experiences at Shanghai and Nanking on My Way Back to China in 1911," in *Hua Qiao and the Hsin Hai Revolution* (Beijing: Chinese Academy of Social Sciences, 1981), 266.
26. *The Chinese of Hawaii-History* (1929), 24.
27. Sun, *Complete Works*, 1:419–422.
28. Hsiang, *Founding Father's Seven Visits*, 134.
29. Jiang, "Study of the Funding," 40-53.
30. *Progress, Australian Monthly* (Melbourne), No. 97 (May 1, 1912).
31. Hsiang, *Founding Father's Seven Visits*, 58.
32. Yansheng Ma Lum, interview with Pang Hong-kwun, May 1998.
33. Sun, *Complete Works*, 1:526.
34. Yansheng Ma Lum, interview with Ching Ping-quon, December 1997.
35. Wen, "Recalling My Work," 218.
36. Ai, *My Seventy Nine Years in Hawaii*, 109.
37. *The Chinese of Hawaii-History* (1929), 24.
38. *The Chinese of Hawaii-History* (1929), 30.
39. Yansheng Ma Lum, interview with Loo Ngan-sum, June 1998.
40. Sun Yat-sen, letter to Francis W. Damon, February 8, 1912.

CHAPTER III

1. Feng, *Unofficial History*, 4:25–37, 63, 64. Feng Tzu-yu's father was an overseas Chinese in Japan and one of the founding members of the Hsing Chung Hui in Yokohama. Feng Tzu-yu met Sun Yat-sen in Yokohama and joined the Hsing Chung Hui when he was only fourteen years old. He later worked very closely with Sun all over the world. He returned to China after the founding of the Republic and became a chronicler documenting material on the revolution.
2. Feng, *Unofficial History*, 4:65.
3. Sun, "Autobiography," 12.
4. Sun, *Complete Works*, 1:463.
5. Most of the photographs accompanying these biographies are reproduced from *The Chinese of Hawaii* (Honolulu, 1929 and 1936). The photographs of Chang Chau, Young Ahin, Young Sen-yat, and Yap Kwai-fong are reproduced courtesy of members of their respective families. The photographs of Sun Mei and Loo Sun are reproduced from *Sun Zhongshan* (Shanghai: Shanghai Museum of Sun Yat-sen's Former Residence, 1996), picture of Soong Kee-yun from *Five Hsing Hui Men of Valor*. The drawings of Chang Kim, Dang Yum-nam, and Chung Mook-heen are by Raymond Lum.
6. Soong and Lin, *Five Hsing Chung Hui Men of Valor*, 168.

7. Feng, *Unofficial History*, 4:29.
8. Yansheng Ma Lum, interview with Ching Ping-quon, Honolulu, December 1997.
9. Feng, *Unofficial History*, 4:30.
10. Feng, *Unofficial History*, 4:29.
11. *The Chinese of Hawaii-Who's Who* (1929), 81; information provided by K. Russell Ho, 1998.
12. Feng, *Unofficial History*, 4:27.
13. Soong and Lin, *Five Hsing Chung Hui Men of Valor*, 165, 166, 167, 172, 175.
14. Hsiang, *Founding Father's Seven Visits*, 36, 37.
15. Irma Tam Soong, "Christian Leaders of the Hsing Chung Hui," paper presented at the International Symposium on Dr. Sun Yat-sen, Founder of the Republic of China, Honolulu, June 11, 1991, 14.
16. Su, "Founding Father's Revolutionary Activities in Hawaii," 78, 79.
17. Soong and Lin, *Five Hsing Chung Hui Men of Valor*, 67.
18. Soong, "Christian Leaders," 14.
19. Feng, *Unofficial History*, 4:37.
20. Ai, *My Seventy Nine Years in Hawaii*, 110, 112.
21. Feng, *Unofficial History*, 4:28.
22. Su, "Founding Father's Revolutionary Activities in Hawaii," 78, 79.
23. *Honolulu Star-Bulletin*, April 29, 1959, 10:1; *Honolulu Advertiser*, April 29, 1959, B9:4.
24. *The Chinese of Hawaii-Who's Who* (1929), 51.
25. *Revolutionary History of the Founding of the Republic of China*, edited by the Da Tong Institute (Taipei, 1929), 1:20.
26. Feng, *Unofficial History*, 4:28; *The Chinese of Hawaii* (1957), 54.
27. Soong and Lin, *Five Hsing Chung Hui Men of Valor*, 185, 189, 191, 204.
28. Feng, *Unofficial History*, 4:4.
29. Soong and Lin, *Five Hsing Chung Hui Men of Valor*, 139, 140, 144, 146, 148, 151.
30. Su, "Founding Father's Revolutionary Activities in Hawaii"; Wen, "Recalling My Work," 229.
31. Feng, *Unofficial History*, 4:63.
32. Hsiang, *Founding Father's Seven Visits*, 88.
33. Feng, *Unofficial History*, 4:37.
34. *The Chinese of Hawaii-Who's Who* (1929), 126; Yansheng Ma Lum, interview with Carolyn Luke, September 1998.
35. Soong, "Christian Leaders," 16.
36. *The Chinese of Hawaii-Who's Who* (1929), 184; *Chinese Hawaii News*, Chinese New Year 1990, 1, 6.
37. Hsing Chung Hui Members and Ledger of Dates and Payments of Membership Fees, Appendix 5.
38. Soong and Lin, *Five Hsing Chung Hui Men of Valor*, 2-14, 23, 34, 54, 60, 61, 63, 68, 72, 73.
39. Soong and Lin, *Five Hsing Chung Hui Men of Valor*, 86, 91, 102, 119, 125, 126.
40. *The Chinese of Hawaii-Who's Who* (1936), 46.

41. *The Chinese of Hawaii-Who's Who* (1936), 47.
42. Feng, *Unofficial History,* 4:58.
43. Char and Char, *Chinese Historical Sites,* 36, 39.
44. Yansheng Ma Lum, interview with Muriel Lai Hip De Ponte, October 1998.
45. Char and Char, *Chinese Historical Sites,* 32.
46. *The Chinese of Hawaii-Who's Who* (1929), 128.
47. Char and Char, *Chinese Historical Sites,* 41, 44.
48. Char and Char, *Chinese Historical Sites,* 50, 51.
49. Feng, *Unofficial History,* 4:177.
50. Yansheng Ma Lum, interview with Veronica Medeiros, May 1988.
51. Su, "Founding Father's Revolutionary Activities in Hawaii," 110-111; Feng, *Unofficial History,* 4:177.
52. Feng, *Unofficial History,* 4:177.
53. Yansheng Ma Lum, interview with Chun Chee-kwon, December 1997.
54. Yansheng Ma Lum, interview with Chee-kwon Chun, May 1998.
55. *The Chinese of Hawaii* (1936), 15; Yansheng Ma Lum, interview with Ching Ping-quon, December 1997.
56. *The Chinese of Hawaii-History* (1929), 26; *The Chinese of Hawaii-Who's Who* (1929),198.
57. *The Chinese of Hawaii-Who's Who* (1929), 30.
58. Yansheng Ma Lum, interview with Owen Loui, December 1997.
59. Wen, "Recalling My Work," 229.
60. *The Chinese of Hawaii-Who's Who* (1936), 18.
61. *The Chinese of Hawaii-Who's Who* (1936), 88.
62. *The Chinese of Hawaii-Who's Who* (1929), 80.
63. *The Chinese of Hawaii-Who's Who* (1929), 86.
64. *The Chinese of Hawaii-History* (1929), 107.
65. *The Chinese of Hawaii, Who's Who* (1936), 52.
66. *The Chinese of Hawaii-Who's Who* (1936), 98.
67. *The Chinese of Hawaii-Who's Who* (1929), 134.
68. *The Chinese of Hawaii-Who's Who* (1929), 136.
69. *The Chinese of Hawaii-Who's Who* (1929), 155.
70. *The Chinese of Hawaii-Who's Who* (1929), 15.
71. *The Chinese of Hawaii-Who's Who* (1929), 177.
72. *The Chinese of Hawaii-Who's Who* (1936), 101.
73. *The Chinese of Hawaii-Who's Who* (1929), 197.
74. *The Chinese of Hawaii-History* (1929), 24.
75. *Honolulu Star-Bulletin,* September 20, 1988.
76. *The Chinese of Hawaii-Who's Who* (1929), 194.
77. Wen, "Recalling My Work," 229.
78. *Dictionary of Overseas Chinese* (Beijing: Beijing University Publishing House, 1993), 347.
79. Yansheng Ma Lum, interview with Leigh-wai Doo, October 1997.
80. *The Chinese of Hawaii-Who's Who* (1929), 206.
81. *The Chinese of Hawaii-Who's Who* (1929), 66.

82. *The Chinese of Hawaii-Who's Who* (1929), 69.
83. *The Chinese of Hawaii-Who's Who* (1929), 102.
84. *The Chinese of Hawaii-Who's Who* (1929), 114.
85. *The Chinese of Hawaii—Who's Who* (1929), 149; Feng, *Unofficial History,* 4:177.

APPENDIX IV

1. According to Soong and Lin, *Five Hsing Chung Hui Men of Valor,* 98, Dang Ying-nam did not attend the first meeting but joined later. According to Hsiang, *The Founding Father's Seven Visits,* 37, Dang Ying-nam did not attend the first meeting and was not elected one of the trustees. Instead, C. K. Ai is listed as one of the trustees.

APPENDIX V

1. This name appears twice: here and below among the entries for April 22, 1895.

GLOSSARY

The Han Yu Pin Yin (Mandarin) spelling is given in parentheses.

Ahmi, S. (Sun Mei) 孫眉
Ai, C. K. [Chung Kun-ai] (Zhong Gong-yu) 鍾工宇
Akana Liili [Tang Kan] (Tang Gen) 唐根
American Chinese Revolutionary Army Fund Raising Bureau, (Meiguo Zhonghua Gemin Jun Chou Xiang Ju) 美國中華革命軍籌餉局
Annam (An-nan) 安南
Apana, L. [Lau Pang] (Liu Pin) 劉聘
Bao Wong Hui (Bao Wang Hui) 保皇會
Canton New Army Uprising (Guangzhou Xin Jun Qiyi) 廣州新軍起義
Chang Chau (Zheng Zhao) 鄭照
Chang Keong (Zheng Qiang) 鄭強
Chang Kim (Zheng Jin) 鄭金
Chang Wing (Zheng Yong) 鄭永
Chee Kung Tong (Zhi Gong Tang) 致公堂
Chee Yow Shin Bo (Zi You Xin Bao) 自由新報
Chen Jiong-ming 陳炯明
Chinese Revolutionary Party Bond (Zhonghua Geming Tang Zhai-juan) 中華革命黨軍債卷
Ching Chow (Cheng Jiu) 程就
Chinlian Uprising (Qinlian Qiyi) 欽廉起義
Ching Nam (Chen Nan) 陳南
Ching Ping-quon (Cheng pin-kun) 程炳焜
Ching Wai-nam (Cheng Wei-nan) 程蔚南
Chiuchou Wong-gang Uprising (Chaozhou Huang-gang Qiyi) 潮州黃崗起義
Chock Chong (Zhuo Xiang) 卓祥
Chock Hoy (Zhuo Hai) 卓海
Chock Lun (Zhuo Ling) 卓麟
Choy Hang village (Cui Heng) 翠亨村
Chun Chee-kwon (Chen Zhi-kun) 陳志昆
Chen K. Moy (Chen Guo-mei) 陳國梅
Chun Shuk-ying (Chen Shu-ying) 陳淑英
Chung Hua Keming Jun (Zhong Hua Geming Jun) 中華革命軍
Chung Hua Keming Tang (Zhong Hua Geming Tang) 中華革命黨
Chung Shan School (Zhong Shan Xue Xiao) 中山學校

Chung Kwok-chee (Zhong Guo-zhu) 鍾國柱
Chung Mook-heen (Zhong Mu-xian) 鍾木賢
Chung Sui-yong (Zhong Shui-yang) 鍾水養
Chung Wun-cheong (Zhong Yun-xiang) 鍾雲祥
Chungkuo Kuomintang (Zhongguo Guomintang) 中國國民黨
Committee to Investigate the Debts of the Hsin Hai Revolution 辛亥革命債務調查委員會

Dang Hu (Deng Fu) 鄧富
Dang Ming-san (Deng Ming-shan) 鄧明山
Dang Sam-park (Deng San-bo) 鄧三伯
Dang Soong-sing (Deng Song-sheng) 鄧松盛
Dang Yum-nam (Deng Yin-nan) 鄧蔭南
Deng Ze-ru (Deng Ze-ru) 鄧澤如
Doo Leigh Wai (Du Li-wei) 杜利威

Fangcheng Uprising (Fangcheng Qiyi) 防城起義
First Canton Uprising (Di Yi Ci Guangzhou Qiyi) 第一次廣州起義

Generalissimo 大元帥
Gold Dollar Banknote (Zhonghua Mingguo Jin-bi) 中華民國金幣

Ha Ah-park (Xia Ya-bo) 夏亞伯
Ha Park-chee (xia Bai-zi) 夏百子
Hee Hon-chew (Xu Han-chao) 許漢超
Hee Jack-son (Xu Zhi-chen) 許直臣
Hee Chiung-chang (Xu Qiong-zhang) 許瓊章
Hee Kwong (Xu Guang) 許廣
Hee Tong (Xu Tang) 許棠
Hekou Uprising (Hekou Qiyi) 河口起義
Ho Fon (He Kuan) 何寬
Ho, K. Russell (He Luo-su) 何羅素

Hoong Moon Fraternity (Hong Men Hui) 洪門會
Hoong Moon Fund Raising Bureau (Hong Men Chou Xiang Ju) 洪門籌餉局
How Ai-chin (Hou Ai-quan) 侯艾泉
Hsing Chung Hui (Xing Zhong Hui) 興中會
Hsin Hai Revolution (Xin Hai Geming) 辛亥革命
Hung Hoy (Hong Hai) 洪海

Kan Wing-chew (Jian Yong-zhao) 簡永照
Kang You-wei 康有為
Ket On Society (Guo An Hui Guan) 國安會館
Kuomintang (Guomingtang) 國民黨
Kwok Min Charity Bureau (Guoming Jiuji Ju) 國民救濟局
Kwong Chong Lung (Guang Chang Long) 廣昌隆

Lai Hip (Li Xie) 黎協
Lai Kwok-ming (Li Guo-ming) 黎國民
Lau Cheong (Liu Xiang) 劉祥
Lau On (Liu An) 劉安
Lau Tang (Liu Deng) 劉登
Lau Yo-ke (Liu Qi-yu) 劉其玉
Lee Chong (Li Chang) 李昌
Lee Chow (Li Qiu) 李秋
Lee Cheng-kao (Li Zheng-gao) 李正高
Lee Duck-sai (Li De-she) 李德社
Lee Gnong-hap (Li Gong-xia) 李公俠
Lee Kai (Li Qi) 李杞
Lee Kwong-fai (Li Guang-hui) 李光輝
Lee Tai-sau (Li Qi-xiu) 李齊秀
Lee To-ma (Li Duo Ma) 李多馬
Leong Hoy (Liang Hai) 梁海
Leong Kwong (Liang Guang) 梁羅光
Liang Chi-chao (Liang Qi-chao) 梁啓超
lishe (Hong Bao) 紅包
Loo Akau (Lu Ah-qiu) 盧阿球
Loo Mu-chun (Lu Mu-zhen) 盧慕貞

GLOSSARY 119

Loo Ngan-sum (Lu Yin-sheng) 盧銀生
Loo Sun (Lu Xin) 盧信
Loo Yuen Aiona (Lu Yuan) 盧源
Loui Kwan-jun (Lei Guan-jin) 雷官進
Lu How-tung (Lu Hao-dung) 陸皓東
Luke Chan (Lu Can) 陸燦
Luke Mun-chan (Lu Wen-can) 陸文燦
Lum Chee (Lin Zhi) 林志
Lum Hong-chee (Lin Kang-xu) 林康敘
Lum Hop (Lin He) 林合
Lum Kam-chin (Lin Jian-quan) 林鑑泉
Lum Kan (Lin Jin) 林近
Lum Mun Kong (Lin Wen Guang) 林文光
Lum, Raymond M. K. 林文光
Lum Wai-icheng (Lin Hui-zeng) 林惠增
Lum Yip Kee (Lin Ye-ju) 林業舉

Mao Man-ming (Mao Wen-ming) 毛文明
Military Bond (Jun Chai Juan) 軍債卷
Ming Sun Yat Bo (Min Sheng Ri Bao) 民生日報

National Fund Raising Bureau (Guoming Juan) 國民捐

Pang Hong-kwun (Peng Feng-qun) 彭鳳群
People's Daily of China (Zhongguo Renming Ri Bao) 中國人民日報

San Ming Zhuyi (San Ming Zhuyi) 三民主義
See Dai Doo Hui Gong (Si Da Du Hui Guan) 四大都會館
Soong Ching Ling (Song Qing-ling) 宋慶齡
Soong Kee-yun (Song Ju-ren) 宋居仁
Soong Shao-kuai (Song Shao-kui) 宋紹逑
Soong Shao-yim (Song Shao-yin) 宋紹殷
Sun Chung Kwok Bo (Xin Zhongguo Bao) 新中國報
Sun Chong (Sun Chang) 孫昌

Sun Fo (Sun Ke) 孫科
Sun On (Sun Wan) 孫琬
Sun Si-wei (Sun Xi-wei) 孫細威
Sun Yuen (Sun Yan) 孫琰
Sun Xia (Sun Xia) 孫霞
Sun Yat-sen, Sun Tai-cheong, Tai Chu (Di Xiang, Sun Wen, Sun Zhong-shan) 孫帝象，孫文，孫逸仙，孫中山
Sun Yat-sen Society, Beijing (Sun Zhong San Xue Hui, Beijing) 北京孫中山學會

Taiping Rebellion 太平天國起義
Tam Ah-fook (Tan Gui-fu) 譚貴福
Tam Kwai (Tan Kui) 譚逵
Tam Wai-gum (Tan Hui-jin) 譚惠金
Tam Yee (Tan Yu) 譚餘
Tan San Sun Bo Loong Kee (Tan Shan Xin Bao Long Ji) 檀山新報隆記
Tao Cheng-chang 陶成章
Tongkin (Dong Jin) 東京
Tung Meng Hui (Tong Meng Hui) 同盟會

Wah Mun School (Hua Wen Xue Xiao) 華文學校
Waichou Uprising (Huizhou Qiyi) 惠州起義
Waichou Chi-nu-hu Uprising (Huizhou Qi-Nu-Hu Qiyi) 惠州七女湖起義
Wen Phong-fei (Wen Xiong-fei) 溫雄飛
Wing Hong Yuen Co. (Yong Hung Yuan Gongsi) 永洪源公司
Wing Wo Tai (Yong He Tai) 永和泰
Mrs. Wong (Huang Er-sao) 王二嫂
Wong But-ting [Wong Lum] (Huang Bi-ting) 黃弼廷
Wong Fa Gong Uprising (Huang Hua Gong Qiyi) 黃花崗起義
Wong Hing-Chow (Huang Qing-zhou) 黃慶洲
Wong Kwon (Wang Kun) 王堃
Wong San-duck (Huang San-the) 黃三德

Wong Wah-fei (Huang Hua-hui) 黃華恢
Wu Jing-heng 吳敬恒
Wu Zhi-hui 吳稚暉

Yap Kwai-fong (Ye Gui-fang) 葉桂芳
Yee Long Wo (Yu Lang-he) 余琅和
Young Ahin (Young Ran) 楊然
Young, Elderly Lady (Yang Tai Fu-ren) 楊太夫人
Young Hook-ing (Yang Fu-rong) 楊福榮
Young Kwong-tat (Yang Guang-da) 楊廣達
Young Mun-nap (Yang Wen-na) 楊文納
Young Sen-yat (Yang Xian-yi) 楊仙逸
Young Tim-Oy (Yang Tian-ai) 楊添靄
Young Wah-duck (Yang Hua-de) 楊華德
Young Zhu-kun (Yang Zhu-kun) 楊著昆
Yuan Shih-kai 袁世凱
Yuan Yim (Yuan Yong) 袁永

Zane Chong-fook (Zeng Zhang-fu) 曾長福
Zhen-nan-guan uprising (Zhen-nan-guan Qiyi) 鎮南關起義

BIBLIOGRAPHY

CHINESE-LANGUAGE PUBLICATIONS

A Chronological Biography of the Founding Father 國父年譜. Taipei: Historical Commission of the Central Committee of the Chinese Kuomintang 中國國民黨黨史編纂委員會編輯出版, 1958.

The Chinese of Hawaii 檀山華僑. Honolulu: Overseas Penman Club 檀山華僑編印社印行, 1929, 1936.

Dictionary of the Hsin Hai Revolution 辛亥革命辭典. Wuhan: Wuhan Publishing House 武漢出版社出版發行, 1991.

Feng Tzu-yu. *Unofficial History of the Revolution* 革命逸史, 馮自由著. Taipei: Taiwan Commercial Press 台灣商務印書館印行, 1965.

Historical Traces of Sun Yat-sen's Activities in Hong Kong, Macao and Overseas 孫中山在港澳與海外活動史蹟. Hong Kong: United College, Chinese University of Hong Kong, and Sun Yat-sen Research Institute, Zhongshan University 香港中文大學和廣州中山大學合編, 1986.

Hsiang Ting-yung. *The Founding Father's Seven Visits to the United States and Hawaii* 國父七訪美檀考述, 項定榮著. Taipei: Time Newspaper and Cultural Publishing Company, Ltd. 台北時報文化出版事業有限公司出版, 1982.

Hua Qiao and the Hsin Hai Revolution 華僑與辛亥革命. Beijing: Chinese Academy of Social Sciences 北京中國社會科學出版社出版, 1981.

Jiang Yung-jing, ed. *Historical Material of Overseas Chinese in the Founding of the Republic* 華僑開國革命史料, 蔣永敬編. Taipei: Zheng Chung Book Store 台北正中書局印行, 1977.

Jiang Yung-jing. "Study of the Funding for the Ten Uprisings Before the Hsin Hai Revolution" 辛亥革命前十次起義經費之研究, 蔣永敬著. In *Historical Material of Overseas Chinese in the Founding of the Republic* 載華僑開國革命史料, 41–56. Taipei: Zheng Chung Book Store 台北正中書局印行, 1977.

Pictorial History of the Republic of China 中華民國史畫. Taipei: Contemporary China Publishing House 台北近代中國出版社出版, 1978.

Pictorial of Mr. Sun Zhong Shan 孫中山先生畫冊. Beijing: Museum of the Chinese Revolution, published by China Culture and History Publishing House 北京中國革命博物館編 中國文史出版社出版, 1986.

Revolutionary History of the Founding of the Republic of China 中華民國革命建國史. Shanghai: Da Tong Institute, published by Xin Guang Book Store 大同學會編輯 上海新光書店發行, 1929.

Su Teh-yung. "The Founding Father's Revolutionary Movement in Hawaii" 國父革命運動在檀島, 蘇德用著文. *In Historical Material of Overseas Chinese in the Founding of the Republic* 載華僑開國革命史料, 57–87.

Sun Yat-sen. *Manuscripts of the Founding Father* 國父墨蹟. Taipei: Historical Commission of the Central Committee of the Chinese Kuomintang, published by Central Supply Agency of Historical and Cultural Material 中央黨史史料編纂委員會編輯中央文物供應社出版, 1950.

———. "Handwritten Auto-Biography" (1896). In *Manuscripts of the Founding Father* 國父墨蹟. Taipei: Historical Commission of the Central Committee of the Kuomintang, published by Chung Hua Publishing Factory 中央黨史史料編纂委員會編輯 中央文物供應社出版, 1961.

———. "Auto-Biography" 自傳. In *San Min Zhuyi* 三民主義. Taipei: Committee of the Million Copies of San Min Zhuyi 三民主義百萬小冊子委員會發行, 1988.

———. *Complete Works of the Founding Father* 國父全集. Taipei: Historical Commission of the Central Committee of the Chinese Kuomintang, published by Central Supply Agency of Historical and Cultural Material 中央黨史史料編纂委員會編輯中華印刷廠承印, 1950.

Sun Zhong Shan 孫中山, ed. *Shanghai Museum of Sun Yat-sen's Former Residence, in Commemoration of the 130th Anniversary of Dr. Sun's Birth* 上海孫中山故居紀念館紀念孫中山先生誕辰 130 周年. Shanghai: Shanghai People's Publishing House 上海人民出版社出版發行, 1996.

Wen Phong-fei. "Recalling My Work With the Tung Meng Hui and Zi You Xin Bao in Hawaii Before 1911" 辛亥前我在檀香山同盟會和自由新報工作的回憶, 溫雄飛著文. In *Hua Qiao and Hsin Hai Revolution* 載華僑與辛亥革命, 223–251. Beijing: Chinese Academy of Social Sciences 北京中國社會科學出版社出版, 1981.

———. "Recalling My Experiences at Shanghai and Nanking on my Way Back to China in 1911" 回憶辛亥時我在歸國途中及在上海和南京親歷親見親聞的事. In *Hua Qiao and the Hsin Hai Revolution* 載華僑與辛亥革命, 252–75.

ENGLISH-LANGUAGE PUBLICATIONS

Ai, C. K. *My Seventy Nine Years in Hawaii.* Hong Kong: Cosmorama Pictorial Publisher, 1960.

At the Call We Gather: Iolani School. Honolulu: Iolani School, 1997.

Char, Tin-Yuke, and Wai Jane Char. *Chinese Historic Sites and Pioneer Families of the Island of Hawaii.* Honolulu: Hawaii Chinese History Center, 1983.

Glick, Clarence E. *Sojourners and Settlers: Chinese Immigrants in Hawaii.* Honolulu: University Press of Hawaii, 1980.

Linebarger, Paul. *Sun Yat-sen and the Chinese Republic.* 1925; reprint New York: AMS Press, 1969.

Mark, Diane Mei Lin. *The Chinese in Kula: Recollections of a Farming Community in Old Hawai.* Honolulu: Hawaii Chinese History Center, 1975.

Restarick, Henry Bond. *Sun Yat-sen: Liberator of China.* New Haven: Yale University Press, 1931.

Schiffrin, Harold Z. *Sun Yat-sen and the Origins of the Chinese Revolution.* Berkeley: University of California Press, 1968.

Soong, Irma Tam. "Christian Leaders of the Hsing Chung Hui." Paper presented at the International Symposium on Dr. Sun Yat-sen, Founder of the Republic of China, Honolulu, June 11, 1991.

Soong, Irma Tam, and Wei-tung Lin. *Five Hsing Chung Hui Men of Valor.* Taipei: Federation of Overseas Chinese Association Publishing House, 1989.

Taylor, Albert Pierce. "Sun Yat Sen in Honolulu." *Paradise of the Pacific,* 38, no. 8 (August 1928):8-11.

Thomsen, Neil L. "No Such Sun Yat-sen: An Archival Success Story." In *Chinese America: History and Perspectives 1997,* 17–26. San Francisco: Chinese Historical Society of America, 1997.

INDEX

Acme Auto Company, Ltd.: 90
Ah Mai Company: 87
Ai, C. K. (Chung Kun): 6, 10, 33, 35, 62, 64, 69, 86; bio., 71
Ai, Steven: 71
Akana, Julia: 16
Akana, L.: *see* Lum Kan
Akana, W.K.: *see* Wong-Gum
All China Women's Federation: xi
American Chinese Army Fund-Raising Bureau: 55, 57
American Congregational Mission: 5
American Theatre (Honolulu): 25

Baldwin family: 16
Baldwin, Peter: 16
Bank of Bishop and Co., Ltd.: 7, 69
Bank of Hawaii: 76
Bao Wong Hui (Save the Monarch Society): 23, 25, 69
Beijing (Peking): vii, xi, 22, 37, 46, 81
Benson, Smith & Company, Ltd.: 86
Berkeley, Calif.: ix
bonds, sale of: 46, 47, 48; Chinese Revolutionary Party bonds, 53, 54, 55; Gold Dollar Banknotes, 58, 59; Hsing Chung Hui bonds, 10, 43, 45; Register of Special Bonds 1893, 44
Boxer Rebellion: 22
Buck Toy: 83

C. Q. Yee Hop & Company: 86
California: 81, 82
Campbell, Calif.: 82
Canada: 11, 31, 46
Cantlie, Dr. James: 20, 21
Canton: 6, 10, 11, 31, 38, 42, 43, 66, 74, 77, 78
Canton New Army Uprising: 31–32, 42
Canton Wong Fa Gong Uprising: 42, 47, 52
Central Bank of China: 72
Chang Chau: 70, 75; bio., 72
Chang Chau, Samuel: 72
Chang Keong: 18, 19, 63
Chang Kim: 68, 75; bio., 70
Chang Wing :83
Chang, Dormant C.: 84
Chee Kung Tong: 30, 41, 50, 51, 56, 57
Chee Yow Shin Bo (Liberty News): ix, 27, 28, 29, 31, 32, 33, 34, 35, 48, 62, 64, 70, 71, 74, 81, 82, 84, 86, 90. *See also Tan San Sun Bo, Ming Sun Yat Bo*
Chen Jiong-ming: 38, 88
Cheong-kong village: 78
Chicago: 31
Chih Pu village: 74

China Daily (newspaper): 71
Chinese air force: 88
Chinese American Bank: 72, 85, 87
Chinese contract laborers: 1
Chinese Embassy (London): 21, 22
Chinese Exclusion Act (1882): 39
Chinese Fire Station (Honolulu): 74
Chinese Free Masons. *See* Chee Kung Tong
Chinese Nationalist Party. *See* Chungkuo Kuomintang
Chinese Revolutionary Army: 21, 25, 26, 34, 59
Chinese Revolutionary Party: 54, 60
Chinese Theater (Honolulu): 31
Chinese-English Debating Society: 9, 19, 27, 75, 76, 78, 85
Ching Chow: 32, 68; bio., 82–83
Ching, Ping-quon: 112
Ching Nam: 10; bio., 71
Ching Wai-nam: 26, 27, 68, 71, 74; bio., 69
Chinlian Uprising: 42
Chiuchou Uprising: 42
Chock Cheong: 64
Chock Hoy: 72
Chock Lun: 43; bio., 84
Choy Hang village, Chung Shan District, Kwangtung Province: 1, 19, 26, 69, 75, 76
Chun Chee-kwon: xi
Chun K. Moy: 84
Chun Shuk-ying: 82
Chung Hua Keming Jun (Chinese Revolutionary Army): 25, 26, 31, 43, 46, 49, 50, 67, 84, 101; members of, 78–81
Chung Hua Keming Tang: 67
Chung Kwok Yi Bo (newspaper): 81
Chung Mook-heen (Chung Kwok-chee) (Chung Sui-yong): 31, 73
Chung Shan District: 69, 72, 78, 83, 84
Chung Shan School: 35, 37, 64, 71, 75, 83, 87
Chungkuo Kuomintang: 67
City Mill Company, Ltd.: 71, 86
College of Medicine (Hong Kong): 6, 20
Committee to Investigate the Debts of the Hsin Hai Revolution: 64
Crabbe, Clarence, Sr.: 69
Curtis Aviation School (Buffalo, N.Y.): 88

Damon, Francis W.: 3, 6, 10, 35, 64, 66; illus., 65
Damon Jr., C. F.: 66
Dan Siang: 64
Dang Hu: 64; bio., 90
Dang Ming-san: 34, 64
Dang Seck-yen: 77

125

126 INDEX

Dang Yum-nam (Dang Soong-sing) (Dang San-po): 8, 9, 10, 11, 43; bio., 77–78
De Ponte, Muriel Lai Hip: 79
Deng Ze-ru: 63
Dr. Sun Yat-sen Hawaii Foundation: vii, viii, 66, 69, 71, 75, 88; formation of, xii
Dr. Sun Yat-sen Institute of Zhong Shan University (Guangzhou): vii
Dutch Indies: *See* Indonesia

Emma Lane, Honolulu: 7, 8
Emma, Queen of Hawaii: 1
En Fon Lee, Mrs.: 45
Eng Brothers Men's Clothing: 34
Eng, Frank: 34
Europe: 11, 31, 46, 58
Ewa, Oahu: 1, 76

Fangcheng Uprising: 42
Feng Tzu-yu: 60, 67
First Canton Uprising: 10–12, 19, 39, 42, 71, 72, 73, 75, 77
First Chinese Church of Christ (Honolulu): 7
Fong Store and the Ching Store: 16
Fort Street Chinese Church School: 76
France: 6
Fukien Province: 58
fund raising: 43–44; accounting of, 62–63; for Canton Wong Fa Gong Uprising, 47; for Waichou Uprising, 45–46

Globe (London newspaper): 20
Goon Tong village: 72, 84
Grannock, S. S. (ship): 3, 18
Guangzhou, China: vii

H. Hackfeld & Company: 75
Ha Park-chee (Ha Ah-park): 10, 12; bio., 73
Hager, Rev. Charles B.: 5
Haleakala Ranch Company: 16
Haleiwa Mission School: 76
Han Ming Bo (newspaper): 85
Hawaiian Contributions to the Ten Uprisings: 42
Hawaiian Evangelical Association: 66
Hee Chiung-chang: 69
Hee Jack-son (Hee Chih-chen): 68; bio., 69–70
Hee Tong: 36; bio., 82
Heen, Harry A.: *see* Chung Mook-heen
Heen, Walter M.: 73
Heen, William H.: 73
Hekou Uprising: 42
Hilo: x, 31, 34, 46, 50, 51, 52, 53, 54, 57, 58, 59, 60, 62, 78, 79, 80
Ho Fon: 7, 8, 27, 49, 67; bio., 69
Ho, K. Russell: 69
Hon-chew: 69
Hong Kong: 5, 6, 11, 20, 22, 27, 43, 45, 46, 50, 51, 52, 62, 67, 70, 71, 73, 74, 77, 81
Honolulu: ix, xii, 6, 7, 8, 9, 10, 18, 19, 20, 21, 23, 24, 25, 26, 27, 31, 32, 33, 34, 35, 39, 43, 48, 49, 50, 62, 64, 66, 69, 70, 71, 72, 73, 74, 75, 76, 78, 81, 82, 83, 84, 85, 86, 87, 88, 90
Honolulu Advertiser (newspaper): 23, 25, 74, 107, 108
Honolulu Iron Works: 82
Hoong Moon Society: 30, 57, 58, 59, 64, 77, 85
Hou Chung-yi: 45

How Ai-chin: 10, 12; bio., 72
Hsiang Ting-yung: 63
Hsing Chung Hui (Revive China Society): vii, xii, xv, 6, 8, 9, 10, 11, 19, 21, 23, 25, 26, 27, 31, 35, 43, 45, 49, 50, 67–68, 81, 97, 98; members of, 68–78
Hsing Chung Hui Memorial Hall: illus, 10
Hua Hsian: 70
Hung Hoy: 85
Hung Kee store: 82
Indochina: 6, 22, 31, 46

Indonesia: xv
Iolani School: vii, 1, 70, 71; illus., 2, 3

Japan: xv, 6, 11, 12, 19, 22, 31, 37, 39, 45, 46, 50, 53, 58, 67, 88
Japanese Theater (Hilo): 24
Jiang Yung-jing: 62

Ka'u, Hawaii: 24
Kaanapali: 73
Kahului, Maui: 5, 18, 71, 74, 77
Kai Ping District: 77
Kailua, Hawaii: 71
Kalakaua, King of Hawaii: vii, 1
Kan Wing-chew: 75
Kang You-wei: 23
Kauai: 73
Keokea, Maui: 5, 16
Ket On Society: 30, 31, 73, 75
Kohala, Hawaii: 72
Korea, S. S. (ship): 39
Kowloon: 77
Kramer, Mac: xi
Kuhio, Prince: 37
Kula Memorial Park: illus., 17
Kula ranch: ix, xii, 12, 13, 16, 19, 63, 70, 77, 83; illus., 14, 15
Kula, Maui: 5, 8, 18, 71
Kuomintang (Nationalist Party): xv, 37, 43, 64, 67, 83, 84, 85, 86
Kwang Cheong Lung store: 33, 34
Kwangsi Province: 58
Kwangtung Province: 1, 11, 12, 38, 39, 58, 73, 74, 77, 78, 88
Kweichow Province: 58
Kwok Min Charity Bureau: *see* Hoong Moon Society
Kwok-ming: *see* Lai Hip
Kwong Chong Loong Company: 83

Lahaina: 73
Lai Hip (Kwok-ming): 24, 34, 46, 50, 51, 52, 53, 54, 55, 62, 79, 80, 105; bio., 79–80
Lai Hip, Herbert: 79
Lau Cheong: 7, 68, 69; bio., 68
Lau Oh: 80
Lau Pang: 34; bio., 91
Lau Ping: 64
Lau Tang: 78
Lau Yo-ke: 78
Lee Cheng-kao: 70
Lee Chong: 7, 8, 9, 68, 74; bio., 70; illus. of home, 8
Lee Chow: 85
Lee Dat-yip: 62
Lee Gnong Hap: 59, 64
Lee Hai Yun: 51

INDEX

Lee Kai: 10; bio., 73
Lee Kwong-fai: 76
Lee Sau Tailor Shop: 91
Lee Say-duck: 70
Lee Tai-sau: 91
Lee To-ma: 45; bio., 70–71
Lee, Frank: 76
Leigh-wai Doo: 88
Leong Doo: 80
Leong Hoy: 64; bio., 82
Leong Kwong: 85
Li, Dr. Min Hin: 84
Lian County: 79
Liang Chi-chao: 23, 24, 80
Liberty Bank: 78, 82, 84
Liberty News: see Chee Yow Shin Bo
Liliuokalani: 1, 70
Lin Jia You, Dr.: vii
Lin, Pearl Sui-ying Sun: 82
Linebarger, Paul: 18
London: 20, 21
Loo Akau: 81
Loo Mu-chun (first wife of Sun Yat-sen): 12, 13, 63
Loo Ngan-sum: 18, 19
Loo Sun: 81
Loo Yuen Aiona: 65
Loong Kee Sun Bo (newspaper): 69, 71; *See also Tan San Sun Bo*
Loui Kwan-jun: 32; bio., 83
Loui, Owen: 32, 83
Lu How-tung: 5, 11, 75
Luke Chan: 9, 12; bio., 75
Luke Chin: 64
Luke Kee store: 90
Luke, Carolyn: 75
Lum Chee (Lum Wai-cheng): x, xi, 36, 47, 64; bio., 80–81; collection of, xi, xii, 46, 50, 55, 57, 59, 62
Lum Hong-chee: 85
Lum Hop: 86
Lum Kam-chin: 71
Lum Kan: 86
Lum, Raymond Mun Kong: xi, 46, 81, 104
Lum Yip Kee: 26, 34
Lum Yip Kee Building: 33
Lum, Elizabeth Lai Hip: 34, 79

Ma Yansheng: xi
Macao: 6, 18, 77, 78
Makawao Elementary School: 19
Makawao, Maui: 18, 70
Malay Peninsula: 50
Manchu dynasty: x, xv, 6, 7, 9, 11, 12, 20, 21, 22, 30, 32, 35, 37, 39, 43, 47, 48, 51, 57, 59, 64, 68, 77; kidnaps Sun Yat-sen, 20; uprisings against, 42
Mao Man-ming: 24; bio., 78–79
Maui: ix, xii, 5, 6, 12, 16, 34, 63, 64, 70, 71, 73, 76, 78
Maui Hua Ren 200 Committee of the Governor's Commission Commemorating the Chinese Bicentennial: 16
Meheula, Mary: 73
Meheula, Solomon: 1
Mei Hu: 88
Mexico: 68, 88
Mills School (Mid-Pacific Institute): 10, 70, 79, 81, 84
Ming Sun Yat Bo (Chinese newspaper): 27, 74, 81. *See also Tan San Sun Bo (Hawaiian Chinese News)*

Mitsubishi Company: 71
Moanalua, Oahu: 78
Molokai: 69, 70, 79
Mongolia, S. S. (ship): 50
Museum of the Chinese Revolution: 81

Nakayama (Japanese name for Sun Yat-sen): 39
Nanking: ix, 37, 62, 64, 75
National Archives: 40
National Fund-Raising Bureau: 62, 87, 88, 90
National Recovery Act: 84
The New Century (French magazine): 62
New York: 20, 31, 35, 58, 63
Ngan-sum Loo (Summie Lum): 65

Oahu: 73
Overseas Chinese Administration Institute of Taiwan: 77
Overseas Penman Club: 84

Palama: 32
Pan Sha, Chung Shan County: 69
Pang Hong-kwun: 18, 63
Peking: *see* Beijing
Penang: 50, 63
People's Daily of China (newspaper): 46, 81, 104
People's Republic of China: 21
Progress (Australian magazine): 62, 63
Punahou School (Oahu College): vii, 3, 72, 75, 83, 93

Republic of China: ix, 12, 19, 21, 35, 37, 38, 43, 58, 59, 60
Revolutionary Army Headquarters: 52, 62
revolutionary organizations. *See* Hsing Chung Hui; Chung Hua Keming Jun; Tung Meng Hui; Kuomintang; Chung Hua Keming Tang; Chungkuo Kuomintang

St. Louis High School (Honolulu): ix, 2, 3, 82, 83
San Bruno, Calif.: 40
San Diego, Calif.: 82
San Francisco: 20, 31, 33, 34, 39, 41, 48, 57, 58, 59, 60, 62, 64
"San Min Zhuyi" (Three Principles of the People): 22, 25
Scotland Yard: 20
Second Revolution: 37
See Dai Doo Society: 26, 27, 75
Sen-yat School: 88
Shanghai: 39, 68, 71, 72, 75
Shanghai Museum of Sun Yat-sen's Former Residence: 39
Shih Jian-ru: 78
Si Wei: 13
Sing Chong Company: 83
Singapore: 31, 50
Sino-American relations: xi
Soong Ching Ling (Madame Sun Yat-sen): xi, 38–39, 88; illus., 89
Soong Kee-yun: 8, 10, 11; bio., 74
Soong Shao-kwai: 74
Soong Shao-yim: 74
South Africa: 67
Southeast Asia: 11, 31, 46, 51, 58
Star-Bulletin (Honolulu newspaper): 72, 84
State Archives of Hawaii: 5
Sun Chong: 77
Sun Chung Kwok Bo (New China Daily News): 23
Sun Chung-shan Society: 46

INDEX

Sun Chung-shan: *see* Sun Yat-sen
Sun Duan: 18
Sun Fo: ix, 12, 13, 28, 45, 64, 77; bio., 82; illus., 30
Sun Mei (S. Ahmi): ix, 1, 3, 5, 6, 8, 9, 12, 13, 16, 18, 19, 23, 39, 43, 63, 70, 75; bankruptcy of, 45; bio., 76–77
Sun On: 13
Sun Tse-ping: 82
Sun Wen: *see* Sun Yat-sen
Sun Xia: 13
Sun Yat-Sen (Sun Wen): xv, 16; admires Hawaii, 5; as a doctor, 12; at medical school, 6; birth, 1; family picture, 13: Fifth visit to Hawaii, 21–30; fourth visit to Hawaii, 12–19; frugality, 63; illus., 5, 13, 30, 38; interest in Christianity, 3; joins Ket On Society, 30; public speeches, 26; returns to China, 35–39; schooling, 1–3; Second visit to Hawaii, 5–6; 16 years of exile, 11; Sixth visit to Hawaii, 31–35; sources of philosophy, 3; Third visit to Hawaii, 6–10
Sun Yat-sen Mall (Honolulu): 9, 10
Sun Yat-sen Memorial Hall (Choy Hang village): 19, 88
Sun Yat-sen Memorial Park: 16
Sun Yat-sen Society: xi, 81
Sun Yuen: 12, 13
Sun, Tse-keong: 82
Szechuan Province: 58

T. Ah Fook Store: 91
Tai Cheong, Tai Chu, Tai Chock: pseudonyms for Sun Yat-sen
Tai Hung Company: 85
Taiping Rebellion: 70
Taiwan: 16, 19, 82
Tam Ah-fook: 91
Tam Cheong: 64
Tam Chi: 64
Tam Kwai: 84
Tam Wai-gum: 81
Tam Yee: 86
Tan San Sun Bo (Hawaiian Chinese News): 24, 26, 28, 69, 71, 74, 75, 81
Tang Kan: 16
Tao Cheng-chang: 62
Tavares, Antone: 16, 19
Tavares, William: 19
Taylor, Albert Pierce: 5, 32, 33, 70
Tchang, Rose Sui-hua Sun: 82
Teng Meng Hui: 36, 43, 49, 102
Tenyo Maru (ship): 71
Thailand: 63
Third Revolution: 38
Thomsen, Neil L.: 39, 40
Tian An Men Square: 46
Tokyo: 11, 23, 25, 31, 39, 50, 60, 67, 71
Tom Shee: 13
Toronto: 50, 51
Triad (secret society): 77
Tung Meng Hui (Alliance Society): ix, xii, xv, 25, 28, 31, 32, 33, 35, 46, 50, 51, 57, 60, 62, 63, 64, 67, 68, 71, 72, 75, 77, 78, 79, 81, 82, 83, 84, 85, 86, 87, 90, 103. *See also* Chinese Revolutionary Army
Tzu You Shin Bo (newspaper): 84

Ulupalakua: 16

UNICEF: xi
United States: 11, 20, 22, 30, 31, 35, 37, 39, 41, 46, 50, 51, 57, 88
United Trust Company: 84
University of Hawaii: ix, 76

Vancouver: 62
Victoria: 50, 51

Wah Mun School: *see* Chung Shan School
Wai-gum, Tom: 49, 50
Waianae, Oahu: 78
Waichou Chi-nu-hu Uprising: 42
Waichou Uprising (1900): 22, 42, 77; funding of, 45–46
Wailuku Poi Factory: 90
Wailuku, Maui: 12
warlords: 37
Wen Phong-fei: 34, 35, 48, 62
Wen Wu Chu Ban She: 46
Whampoo: 77
Wilcox, Robert William: 74
Wing Chong Loong Company: 83, 86
Wing Hong Yuen Company: 32, 82
Wing Wo Tai (store): 7, 68
Wong But-ting: 87
Wong Er-sao: 63
Wong Fa Gong Uprising: *see* Canton Wong Fa Gong Uprising
Wong Gum (W.K. Akana): 24, 55, 61, 79, 80; bio., 80
Wong Hing-chow: 86
Wong Kwon: 88
Wong San-duck: 30
Wong Wah-fei: 68
Wong, Harriet (Pak Hoy): 12
Wu Hua, Kwangtung Province: 73
Wu Jing-heng (Wu Zhi-hui): 45, 62
Wuchang Uprising: 12, 35, 58, 59, 74
Wun Cheong: 73

Yan Sen: 62
Yansheng: xi
Yap Chau: 64
Yap Kwai-fong: 9; bio., 76
Yat Go Mien restaurant: 63
Yat Sing Cheong Company: 88
Yat Sing dry-goods store: 87
Yee Long Wo: 87
Yee Shun Kee Dry Goods Store: 86
Young Ahin: 62, 88; bio., 87–88
Young Hook-ing: 62; bio., 87
Young Kwong-tat: 33, 35, 49, 62; bio., 83
Young Mun-nap: 1; bio., 75
Young Sen-yat: 88
Young Tim-oy: 88
Young Wah-duck: 33, 35, 49, 83
Yuan Shih-kai: 37, 38, 74
Yuan Yim: 90
Yunan Province: 58

Zane Chong-fook: 27, 35, 64; bio., 74–75
Zhen-nan-guan Uprising: 42
Zhen-nan-guan, battle of: 6
Zhongshan County: vii